"Ray's expertise in the BBQ industry is smokin'. This is a must-read from one of the best in the trade. You will love the knowledge he brings."

—BARBARA LATIMER, president, National Barbecue and Grilling Association

"Ray Sheehan's expert knowledge and indispensable guidance will help you get the most out of your Big Green Egg®. I am thrilled to learn from this barbecue master."

—JIMMY CARBONE, founder of Sauce King NYC

"Ray Sheehan is a true guru of barbecue and grilling who you can trust with all manner of smoked meats and tasty sauces. Both beginners and veterans of the Big Green Egg® will love this book."

—SEAN LUDWIG, co-founder of The Smoke Sheet and founder of NYC BBQ

"Ray's new book gives the novice enthusiast a solid foundation in kamado-style cooking, and his recipes will inspire even the most seasoned Egghead! I can't wait to try these recipes in my backyard."

—RYAN COOPER, founder of BBQ Tourist and co-founder of The Smoke Sheet

"Ray is an expert cook who shares the knowledge, insights and techniques necessary to create wonderful dishes and ensure success every time you fire up the Big Green Egg®."

—TIM O'KEEFE, Kansas City Barbeque Society judge and cookbook coauthor

"Whether you're a Big Green Egg® novice or an expert pitmaster, Ray's book will become your go-to for all things Big Green Egg®."

—VIC CLEVENGER, founder of Chimney Cartel

"In his new book, Ray tackles the home BBQ aficionado's holy grail, the renowned Big Green Egg®. Eminently readable and chock-full of tips, tricks and techniques to take anyone from novice to master. Absolutely a must-read for the kamado crowd!"

—JOHN COHL, culinary entertainment radio and podcast host

"Ray's got that touch that keeps a recipe feeling like comfort food but with flairs that make them stand out among your guests and tailgaters—and most importantly, on your taste buds."

—JANE EHRHARDT, food & drink editor, *Tailgater Magazine*

BIG GREEN EGG® BASICS

From a MASTER BARBECUER

RAY SHEEHAN

Author of *Award-Winning BBQ Sauces
and How to Use Them*

PAGE STREET
PUBLISHING CO.

PAGE STREET
PUBLISHING CO.

First published in 2022 by
Page Street Publishing Co.
27 Congress Street, Suite 1511
Salem, MA 01970
www.pagestreetpublishing.com

Distributed by Macmillan, sales in Canada by The Canadian Manda Group.

26 25 24 23 22   1 2 3 4 5

The "Big Green Egg" is a registered trademark of Big Green Egg, Inc.

ISBN-13: 978-1-64567-476-4
ISBN-10: 1-64567-476-2

Library of Congress Control Number: 2021938437

Cover and book design by Julia Tyler for Page Street Publishing Co.
Photography by Ken Goodman

Printed and bound in the United States

For my wife, Kelly

The most amazing parts of my life have not just been beside you, they have also been because of you. Through the years we have accomplished so much together, but it has been your unyielding support that has made my barbecue dreams, and many others, a reality. I am blessed to have such an incredible woman as my biggest fan and loudest cheerleader. Thank you for always believing in me and loving me the way that you do.

I love you.

Contents

Introduction

If this book caught your attention, then it is probably safe to assume that you are an outdoor cooking enthusiast who would like to learn about kamado-style cooking. When it comes to kamado-style cooking, the Big Green Egg® is billed as "The Ultimate Cooking Experience." That is because it is one of the most versatile and durable cookers on the market today. Feel like searing some steaks over direct heat? Slow smoking your favorite barbecue meats? How about creating brick oven–like pizza and baked goods? The Big Green Egg can do it! With its egg shape and thick ceramic walls, this kamado-style cooker can maintain a steady, even heat, helping you achieve great results right away. With some knowledge and a little practice, you will learn how to grill, smoke, roast and bake like a pro in your own backyard.

What makes me think I can help you? Well, I was you. I have been on a quest to learn all that I can about barbecuing for the better part of my adult life. What started out as experimentation with a kettle-style charcoal grill has grown into an all-out obsession with outdoor cooking and a growing arsenal of smokers, grills and kamado-style cookers. In 2014, this obsession led me to get involved in competition barbecue. Since then, my BBQ Buddha Competition team has competed head to head with some of the top pitmasters in the country. We have gotten top ten calls in such categories as chicken, ribs, pork, brisket, bacon, chili and even crab cakes. Around the same time, I began creating the sauces and rubs that we would use to flavor our 'cue. They were so well received at cookouts, family gatherings and on the barbecue circuit that I decided to make a go of it as a business. The BBQ Buddha brand was born! Soon after creating this all-natural line of BBQ sauces and rubs, the awards started coming in, but this time for the sauces themselves. My BBQ sauces have received top honors

at some of the biggest national and international competitions, such as the American Royal "Best Sauce on the Planet" contest, the National Barbecue and Grilling Association's Awards of Excellence, the Scovie Awards, the World Hot Sauce Awards, the International Flavor Awards (the Flaves) and the Sauce King NYC Championship. I also authored *Award-Winning BBQ Sauces and How to Use Them: The Secret Ingredient to Next-Level Smoking*, which won BBQ Book of the Year from both the National Barbecue & Grilling Association and *Barbecue News Magazine* for 2020.

Over the years, my business has grown to include teaching barbecue cooking classes, pop-up dinners and speaking engagements. I am proud to be a part of this barbecue community and thoroughly enjoy sharing my experiences, tips and best techniques for grilling and smoking to preserve the barbecue culture and pass it on to the next generation of cooks and pitmasters.

If you are seeking a solid foundation in kamado-style cooking, then you are in the right place. In this book I will cover everything you need to get started, including how a ceramic cooker works, lighting the fire, temperature control and more. With 60 standout recipes, and chapters that are organized by technique, you will become familiar with every aspect of cooking on the Big Green Egg. It won't be long before you master these recipes and begin creating your own. Are you ready to crack open the Big Green Egg and take your grilling and smoking to the next level? Let's go!

Ray Sheehan

GETTING STARTED

HOW A CERAMIC COOKER WORKS

Kamado-style cooking is extremely versatile and allows you to use such techniques as "hot and fast" with direct grilling, "low and slow" for smoking, as a "convection" oven for roasting or baking and even as a high-temperature pizza oven. Its airtight cooking chamber helps keep food moist as it cooks. In fact, the secret to achieving great results when cooking on a kamado centers on three things: heat retention, airflow and temperature control. For this reason, I recommend that you cook primarily with the lid closed. This will allow the heat to radiate inside the Big Green Egg (a.k.a. EGG) and keep moisture from escaping. Kamados are also extremely economical when it comes to fuel consumption. A single load of charcoal can last eighteen-plus hours, depending on what size cooker and lump charcoal you have, while holding a constant temperature.

The word *kamado* comes from a Japanese term that translates into "stove" or "cooking range." It is a style of cooking that dates back over 3,000 years, which features a circular clay or ceramic vessel that uses wood and/or charcoal as its fuel to cook the food. Traditionally, clay pots were used in this style of cooking due to their heat retention properties and their ability to prevent food from losing excess moisture as it is cooked.

Since its invention, the kamado-style grill has come a long way. Producers of these modern ceramic cookers, such as the Big Green Egg, have taken advantage of advances in ceramic formulas, which have resulted in a much more durable product. Their thick ceramic walls retain heat and moisture to produce results far superior to metal grills and smokers.

OVERVIEW OF THE BIG GREEN EGG

Components

The Big Green Egg is available in seven different sizes, ranging from 2XL all the way down to Mini, and they are all set up in the same style. The egg shape of the cooker is designed to contain the heat by using two draft doors, one in the bottom of the base and another at the top in the dome.

Available Big Green Egg Sizes:

- 2XL 29-inch (74-cm) diameter for a total cooking area of 672 square inches
- XLarge 24-inch (61-cm) diameter for a total cooking area of 452 square inches
- Large 18.25-inch (46-cm) diameter for a total cooking area of 262 square inches
- Medium 15-inch (38-cm) diameter for a total cooking area of 177 square inches
- Small 13-inch (33-cm) diameter for a total cooking area of 133 square inches
- MiniMax 13-inch (33-cm) diameter for a total cooking area of 133 square inches
- Mini 10-inch (25-cm) diameter for a total cooking area of 79 square inches

Base—Lower Draft Door

Gasket

Temperature Gauge

Base—Lower Draft Door: There are two layers to the bottom draft door: the door itself and a mesh screen to keep ash and embers from falling out of the cooker. Be sure that the mesh screen is closed while running your EGG.

The bottom draft door slides horizontally to control air flow. Think of this draft door as being used for major temperature control of more than 10°F (5.5°C) at a time.

Gasket: The kamado felt gasket provides an airtight seal between the lid and the base when closed. This is important both for the moisture retention and to ensure that the air flow through the kamado operates as it should.

Dome—Upper Draft Door and Daisy Wheel: The upper draft door, or daisy wheel, swivels left and right, creating updraft, and in turn adjusting the temperature used in the cook.

The upper vent is more of a minor temperature control, which is used when you are trying to dial in a temperature less than 10°F (5.6°C). The upper vent setting consists of a cast-iron vent that has a dual function. The dual-variable daisy wheel allows for precise temperature control. If you are within a few degrees, you just need to adjust the top daisy wheel, and if you are within 5 to 10°F (2.8 to 5.6°C), you can adjust the lower daisy wheel. If you have a rEGGgulator cap, you can make one adjustment to dial in your temperature.

Temperature Gauge: Registers the temperature in the cook chamber at the top of the dome.

The Firebox: Holds your fuel and is constructed with a cutout that must line up with the bottom vent of the EGG to allow air to enter and feed the flame.

Fire Grate: The fire grate rests in the base of the fire box. It is a heavy, cast-iron part with holes that allow incoming air through to the fire.

Fire Ring: The fire ring sits on top of the fire box. It creates the space for your charcoal to burn in. The fire ring and the fire box make up the lining of the EGG's interior, where the fire gets the hottest. It also creates the surface for the heat diffuser and cooking grate to rest on.

Cooking Grid: The cooking grid is where you do the cooking. It sits atop the fire ring when using direct heat or atop the heat diffuser when cooking with an indirect heat setup.

Pizza Stone

REGGulator Cap

Plate Setter

Accessories

IntEGGrated Nest Handler and Acacia Hardwood Tables: Both of these will do a fine job of holding your EGG securely while you cook.

EGG Mates: These wooden side shelves are practical and have great eye appeal.

ConvEGGtor, a.k.a. the Plate Setter: This heat diffuser is the most important accessory for going low and slow on the EGG. It forms a barrier between the fire and the food you are cooking.

EGGspander: A multilevel rack that gives you the ability to cook more food at the same time.

Pizza Stone: A ceramic baking stone that distributes heat for even baking and browning.

Cast-Iron Plancha Griddle: Ideal for searing meats, cooking seafood, sautéing vegetables and grilling sandwiches and panini.

REGGulator Cap: Cast-iron vent cap that replaces the traditional dual-function metal top. Unlike its predecessor, the rEGGulator does not move upon opening the EGG once you have your temperature dialed in.

Automatic Draft System Control, such as EGG Genius or BBQ Guru DigiQ: If you are having trouble controlling your temperature, these draft systems can make your EGG a set-it-and-forget-it cooker.

TOOLS I CAN'T LIVE WITHOUT

- Heat-resistant barbecue gloves
- Nitrile gloves with cotton glove liners
- Instant-read thermometer, such as a ThermoWorks
- Natural lump charcoal, such as Fogo, Jealous Devil or Big Green Egg brands
- Good sharp knives, such as Gunter Wilhelm brand
- Cast-iron cookware, such as Lodge brand

- Fire starters
- Ash tool
- Ash can
- Disposable cutting boards
- Grill brush
- Long-handled basting brush
- Metal spring-loaded tongs
- Spatula
- Lighter

Direct   *Indirect with Drip Pan*   *Indirect without a Drip Pan*

COMMON EGG SETUPS

Method: Direct

This is the most common setup and is used for direct cooking, searing and high-heat grilling. Load your firebox to the top with natural lump charcoal. Light it and replace the cooking grid.

Method: Indirect with a Drip Pan

This method of indirect cooking is typically used for smoking or roasting. By adding a convEGGtor (heat diffuser), you now have a barrier between the direct heat and the food. The drip pan will catch any of the dripping fat and prevent it from burning on the heat diffuser. For this setup, fill the firebox to the top with natural lump charcoal, layering it with smoking wood chunks if you are using them. Light the charcoal, and once the fire is lit, put in the convEGGtor with the legs pointing up, top it with the drip pan and replace the cooking grid.

Method: Indirect without a Drip Pan

This method of indirect cooking is great for roasting and baking foods that are going to be cooked in a pan or do not drip. It is the same setup as indirect with a drip pan, minus the drip pan.

CHOOSING THE RIGHT FUEL

I recommend using natural hardwood lump charcoal in your EGG for a cleaner, hotter burn. Briquettes can be full of chemicals and produce a lot of ash. More ash means that you are burning through your fuel at a faster rate. An excessive amount of ash in a kamado-style grill will block the airflow, resulting in a drop in temperature or even a dead fire.

LIGHTING THE FIRE

Building a fire in your EGG for the first time can seem a bit intimidating, but it really is a fairly simple process. There are several methods for lighting, but whatever you do, don't use lighter fluid! Not only will it give your food an off taste, but it can seep into the pores of the ceramic and that chemical smell will be difficult to get out of your cooker for some time.

Most people start their EGG using a torch or fire starters. I prefer to use natural charcoal starters: small, square, flat pieces of paraffin and sawdust. I break them in half so that the edges are easier to light.

Fire Starters Being Lit

To start your EGG: Load your charcoal to the top of the firebox at the bottom of the fire ring. Place three of the starter halves in a triangular pattern, just tucking them under the lump so that they are evenly spaced, starting at the rear of the firebox. Light the fire starters, then after a few minutes, add the convEGGtor (heat diffuser), if using it, and then replace the cooking grid. At this point, the bottom draft vent and lid should be left open. After seven to ten minutes, close the bottom draft screen and the lid to the EGG, leaving the bottom draft vent and top vents wide open for a few more minutes before making any adjustments.

TEMPERATURE CONTROL

Begin working toward your desired cooking temperature. Note the temperature at the dome and adjust your vents accordingly. You may have to close the top and bottom vents up to 50 percent at this time, then make only minor adjustments as necessary. The ceramic inside of the EGG is such a great insulator that if you overshoot your target temperature, it will take some time to get it back down; therefore, you want to try to creep up on it slowly.

Using your dampers to control the airflow through your EGG will help you dial in your desired cooking temperature. If you want to raise the temperature in your EGG, add more air by opening the vents. If you want to cool the EGG down, reduce the amount of airflow to the fire by closing the vents. Give your cook temperature a chance to settle without making too many adjustments all at once.

The Big Green Egg setup instructions listed in each recipe include an approximate measure, listed as a percentage, for how wide to open your vents during cooking. Use this chart as a guide, then make adjustments to dial in your cook temperature as necessary.

Desired Cook Temperature	Vents Open %
250°F (120°C)	10%
275°F (140°C)	15%
300°F (150°C)	20%
325°F (170°C)	25%
350°F (180°C)	30%
375°F (190°C)	35%
400°F (200°C)	40%
425°F (225°C)	50%
450°F (230°C)	60%
500°F (250°C)	65%
600°F (315°C)	75%

If this is the first cook on your new Big Green Egg, I do not recommend cooking at a high temperature. This may damage the gasket before it can properly seal itself. Instead, light your cooker and bring the temperature up to 350°F (180°C) for three hours, to allow the gasket adhesive to fully cure and adhere to the EGG, before cooking at higher temperatures.

Calibrate your dome thermometer regularly to maintain accurate cooking temperatures. To do this, carefully take the thermometer out of the dome and, using a ⁷⁄₁₆-inch (11-mm) wrench or a pair of pliers, grab the nut on the back of the dial. Place the tip of the thermometer, by at least 1 inch (2.5 cm), into boiling water and see whether it reads 212°F (100°C). If it does not, hold the dial and rotate it until it reads 212°F (100°C).

ASH MANAGEMENT

When you are done cooking, simply close the top and bottom draft vents to cut off air to the firebox and extinguish the fire. The EGG will remain hot for several hours. Allow it to cool completely before attempting to remove the ash.

When you are ready to do your next cook, remove the cooking grid and convEGGtor and set them aside. Stir the remaining coals with your ash tool, allowing the spent ash to drop to the bottom of the EGG. Insert the ash tool into the bottom vent door and scrape out the ash into a small metal ash can fitted with a lid. Reload your firebox with fresh charcoal and stir to combine it before lighting.

Ash Tool

SAFETY

One of the many things that people love about cooking on a charcoal grill is that they get to cook with live fire. While cooking on the EGG is not dangerous, taking simple but necessary precautions will ensure a safe and fun grilling experience.

Avoiding Backdraft/Flashback

A backdraft, or a flashback as it is sometimes referred to, happens when you quickly shut off oxygen to a hot fire, then quickly reintroduce it. Flashback is more likely to occur when you are cooking above 350°F (180°C), but can still happen at lower temperatures. This is easily managed by "burping" your EGG as you open it. To "burp" your EGG, slowly lift the dome a couple of inches (at least 5 cm) and hold it there for a few seconds, then slowly open it all the way.

Preventing Flare-Ups

Use a drip pan when smoking or roasting to prevent flare-ups. Flare-ups are essentially grease fires that happen when excessive dripping fat and the juices of cooking meat come into contact with the heat diffuser or the hot coals of your fire. Never use water to put out a grease fire. You can shut it down by closing the top and bottom vents on your cooker, thus cutting off oxygen to the fire.

MAINTAINING YOUR EGG

Nuts and Bolts of It

Periodically inspect all fasteners, nuts and bolts for tightness. The metal bands on the EGG are designed to keep the dome of your EGG secure. Check the tightness of these fittings after the first few uses, and then at least twice a year. In addition to the band and hinge hardware, all nuts and bolts should be checked regularly for proper operation and tightness.

Clean as You Go

Keeping your grill clean not only produces better-tasting food, but also helps extend its life. Never use chemical cleaners or water inside of your EGG, as they could get inside of the pores in the ceramic and leach into your food. For easy cleanup, I recommend wrapping your convEGGtor in heavy-duty aluminum foil. If your cooker is particularly dirty from your most recent cook, don't worry. Your kamado-style cooker acts as a self-cleaning oven.

After each cook, close the lid on the EGG and let it continue to burn for about fifteen minutes. Then, using a grid tool or steel mesh brush, scrape the stainless-steel grid to remove any remaining stuck-on food particles and prevent buildup on the cooking grid.

A couple of times a year, or as needed with frequent use, you may want to raise the temperature in your EGG and do a clean burn. While it is not required, it is a good idea to give your cooker a good deep cleaning to rid it of any fat, grease or leftover debris. To deep clean your EGG, remove any leftover charcoal from your previous cook. Load the EGG with fresh charcoal to the top of the fire ring and light it. Replace the convEGGtor and stainless-steel grid. You can also put the daisy wheel on the grid to clean, if necessary. Close the lid, open the bottom vent wide and get your cooker up to 600°F (315°C) for about an hour. Close the bottom vent and allow the grill to cool completely. This may take four to five hours. With a stainless-steel brush, scrape away any residue and buildup. Use an ash tool to stir up the coals and remove the ash.

Replacing the Gasket

The heat-sealing gasket material installed on your Big Green Egg is designed to last for years under normal operating conditions. However, if the gasket shows signs of excessive wear and deterioration, or smoke is visibly seeping from where the lid and base meet, it is time to replace it. Once the cooker is completely cool, use a putty knife to scrape and remove the old gasket, as well as any grease or built-up residue. Use a rag that has been dipped in acetone to remove any of the leftover adhesive and finish cleaning before applying the new gasket. Next, light your EGG and bring the temperature up to around 350°F (180°C) for three hours to allow the gasket adhesive to fully cure and adhere to the EGG before cooking at higher temperatures.

Hot 'n' Fast

SEARING, DIRECT GRILLING

Direct cooking is what most people think of when it comes to backyard grilling. This technique is great for smaller, quick-cooking items, such as burgers, steaks, chops, chicken breasts, fish and vegetables. The food is cooked directly over hot coals, with temperatures ranging anywhere from 300 to 500°F (150 to 250°C). When you fire up your grill, make sure you have an even bed of hot coals so that you maintain a steady even heat throughout the cook.

The key to achieving a great sear is to start with a clean, hot grill and well-oiled grates or cast-iron pan. Get your grill hot, then drizzle some olive oil onto a paper towel and use a pair of long metal tongs to rub down the cooking grate. As the meat cooks, it will release from the grid and you will know it is time to turn it.

An advantage of direct grilling on the EGG is its ability to sear a flavorful crust on the exterior of the meat while keeping the interior moist and juicy. As the meat cooks over the hot fire, its protein and natural sugars caramelize, creating that char-grilled flavor that we all crave.

In this chapter, we will grill such dishes as the Coffee-Rubbed New York Strip Steaks with Chimichurri sauce (page 24), Asian-Style Pork Burgers with Crunchy Slaw and Yum Yum Sauce (page 36) and Skirt Steak Fajitas (page 32) and sear such dishes as the Seared Porterhouse Steak for Two (page 27), Seared Scallops over Warm Corn Salad (page 40) and Seared Ahi Tuna with Lemon Caper Vinaigrette (page 44). I will show you the secret to making my Award-Winning Maryland-Style Crab Cakes (page 48) on the Big Green Egg, and so much more. Fire up the grill and let's get cooking!

Coffee-Rubbed New York Strip Steaks with Chimichurri

Makes about 4 servings

This Argentinean-inspired steak dish features a seasoning rub that is laced with coffee and chiles, giving it a robust and earthy flavor. When grilling these steaks over the hot coals in your EGG, you will feel as though you have been transported to a South American steak house without having to leave the comfort of your own backyard.

ANCHO ESPRESSO RUB

2 tbsp (15 g) ancho chile powder

2 tbsp (30 g) finely ground espresso

2 tbsp (30 g) dark brown sugar

1 tbsp (7 g) smoked paprika

1½ tsp (9 g) kosher salt

1½ tsp (2 g) dried oregano

1½ tsp (9 g) freshly ground black pepper

1½ tsp (3 g) ground coriander

1½ tsp (4 g) dry mustard

1 tsp New Mexico red chile powder

1 tsp ground ginger

CHIMICHURRI

¼ cup (60 ml) sherry vinegar

¼ cup (60 ml) red wine vinegar

2 tbsp (30 ml) extra-virgin olive oil, plus more for steaks

½ tsp sugar

1 shallot, chopped

¼ cup (15 g) fresh parsley, chopped

3 cloves garlic, chopped

¼ cup (4 g) fresh cilantro, chopped

1 tbsp (3 g) chopped fresh chives

1 tsp dried oregano

Kosher salt

Freshly ground black pepper

4 (10- to 12-oz [280- to 340-g]) New York strip steaks

Prepare the rub: In a medium-sized bowl, stir together all the rub ingredients, then set aside. Leftover rub may be stored in an airtight container for up to 6 months.

Prepare the chimichurri: In a blender, combine the vinegars, olive oil, sugar, shallot, parsley, garlic, cilantro, chives and oregano. Blend until smooth. Season with salt and black pepper to taste. Let stand for 20 minutes.

Set up the EGG for 450°F (230°C) direct grilling. Fill your firebox with natural lump charcoal, and with the top and bottom vents wide open, light the fire and close the EGG. After about 10 minutes, close the bottom draft screen. When the temperature nears your 450°F (230°C) target temperature, partially close the bottom vent door and the top of the daisy wheel, leaving both vents 50 percent open. Make minor adjustments as necessary.

Once the EGG comes up to temperature, apply the rub to your steaks and place them on the grill, then cook for about 4 minutes. If you want to achieve great-looking crosshatch grill marks, rotate the steaks 90 degrees after 2 minutes. Flip the steaks and continue to cook for about 4 minutes more, or until the meat reaches 130°F (54°C) for medium rare or your preferred doneness. Transfer the steaks to a plate and let rest for 10 minutes.

Slice the steaks and arrange on a platter to serve. Spoon some of the chimichurri onto the meat and pass the remaining sauce around the table.

SEARED PORTERHOUSE STEAK FOR TWO

Makes 2 servings

Often referred to as the king of steaks, the porterhouse is the perfect combination of sirloin (New York strip) and tenderloin (filet mignon). It's the best of both worlds. This is the ultimate steak for sharing.

The secret to steak perfection on the Big Green Egg is having the ability to pan sear and oven finish, all on one cooker. This gives your steak a nicely seared exterior, with a juicy and tender interior.

1 (24- to 30-oz [680- to 850-g]) porterhouse steak, 1½" to 2" (2.5 to 5 cm) thick

Kosher salt

Freshly ground black pepper

2 tbsp (30 ml) grapeseed oil

¼ cup (55 g/½ stick) salted butter

3 sprigs thyme

3 sprigs rosemary

3 cloves garlic, crushed with the back of a knife

The first step to achieving the most amazing golden-brown crust is to remove excess moisture from the exterior of the steak. Pat the steak dry, then season it liberally with salt and pepper. Let it sit out at room temperature for 30 minutes before cooking.

Set up the EGG for 500°F (250°C) direct grilling. Fill your firebox with natural lump charcoal, and with the top and bottom vents wide open, light the fire and close the EGG. After about 10 minutes, close the bottom draft screen. When the temperature nears your 500°F (250°C) target temperature, partially close the bottom vent door and the top of the daisy wheel, leaving both vents 65 percent open. Make minor adjustments as necessary.

Place a large, cast-iron skillet on the cooking grid to preheat for about 20 minutes. Heat the oil until it shimmers in the skillet. Place the steak in the skillet and cook for 2 to 3 minutes. Flip the steak, close the lid and continue to cook for 2 to 3 minutes more. Using heatproof gloves, tilt the pan and add the butter, thyme, rosemary and garlic. Continue to cook, basting the steak constantly, until it reaches an internal temperature of 125°F (52°C) for medium rare, about 4 minutes, or until your desired doneness.

Transfer the steak to a platter and allow it to rest for 5 minutes. Strain the pan juices and pour them over the steak to serve.

Porcini-Crusted Rib-Eye Steaks
with Black Garlic Butter

Makes 2 to 4 servings

These steaks are layered with savory umami flavor—first in the mushroom crust, and then in the finishing butter—that keeps you coming back for more. The fermented black garlic lends a sweet molasses-like richness with tangy garlic undertones that complement the natural flavor of the beef.

BLACK GARLIC BUTTER

½ cup (112 g/1 stick) unsalted butter, at room temperature

1 tbsp (3 g) fresh thyme leaves

1 tsp Worcestershire sauce

Zest of 1 lemon

4 cloves black garlic, minced

Kosher salt

Freshly ground black pepper

STEAKS

1 (½-oz [15-g]) package dried porcini mushrooms

2 boneless rib-eye steaks, 1½" (4 cm) thick

Kosher salt

Freshly ground black pepper

Prepare the black garlic butter: In a medium-sized bowl, combine the butter, thyme, Worcestershire sauce, lemon zest and garlic, plus salt and pepper to taste. Using a spoon or silicone spatula, place the butter mixture on a piece of plastic wrap and roll it into the shape of a log. Twist the ends to seal, then refrigerate for 1 hour, or until ready to use.

Prep the steaks: In a spice grinder, process the dried porcini mushrooms to a fine powder. Transfer to a plate and set aside. Season the steaks with an even layer of salt and pepper, then press them into the mushroom powder to coat both sides well. Allow the steaks to sit at room temperature for 30 minutes, or until the grill is ready to cook.

Set up the EGG for 500°F (250°C) direct grilling. Fill your firebox with natural lump charcoal, and with the top and bottom vents wide open, light the fire and close the EGG. After about 10 minutes, close the bottom draft screen. When the temperature nears your 500°F (250°C) target temperature, partially close the bottom vent door and the top of the daisy wheel, leaving both vents 65 percent open. Make minor adjustments as necessary.

Once the EGG comes up to temperature, place the steaks on the cooking grid, leave the lid open and cook for 2 minutes. Rotate the steaks 90 degrees and cook for 2 minutes more. Flip the steaks and close the lid. Continue to cook until the steaks reach an internal temperature of 125°F (52°C) for medium rare, about 4 minutes, or until your desired doneness.

Transfer the steaks to a platter and top each steak with a slice of the black garlic butter. Allow the steaks to rest for 4 to 5 minutes before serving.

Note: Black garlic is available in many specialty grocers. My favorite comes from Black Garlic Market in Pensacola, Florida.

Hoisin-Glazed Pork Chops

Makes 4 servings

Give these pork chops a base layer of flavor by rubbing the Chinese five-spice powder and other spices into the meat before they hit the grill. Cooking them hot and fast on the EGG with the lid closed will ensure that they stay tender and moist. Brush the chops with the hoisin glaze during the last five minutes of cooking, for an exotic, sweet and spicy finish.

HOISIN GLAZE

½ cup (120 ml) soy sauce

½ cup (120 ml) ketchup

½ cup (110 g) light brown sugar

¼ cup (60 ml) dry sherry

2 cloves garlic, chopped

¼ cup (60 ml) honey

3 tbsp (45 ml) hoisin sauce

2 tsp (4 g) grated fresh ginger

½ tsp red pepper flakes

2 tbsp (12 g) Chinese five-spice powder

4 bone-in center-cut pork chops, 1½" (4 cm) thick

2 tsp (5 g) granulated garlic

Kosher salt

Freshly ground black pepper

Set up the EGG for 400°F (200°C) direct grilling. Fill your firebox with natural lump charcoal, and with the top and bottom vents wide open, light the fire and close the EGG. After about 10 minutes, close the bottom draft screen. When the temperature nears your 400°F (200°C) target temperature, partially close the bottom vent door and the top of the daisy wheel, leaving both vents 40 percent open. Make minor adjustments as necessary.

Prepare the glaze: In a small saucepan, combine all the glaze ingredients. Simmer over medium-low heat for 8 to 10 minutes, stirring occasionally, or until the sauce has slightly thickened. Keep warm until ready to use.

Sprinkle the Chinese five-spice powder over the pork chops and rub it into the meat. Season the chops with the granulated garlic, salt and black pepper.

Once the cooker comes up to temperature, place the chops on the cooking grid and close the lid. Cook for about 4 minutes. If you want to achieve great-looking crosshatch grill marks, rotate the chops 90 degrees after 2 minutes. Flip the pork chops and continue to cook for about 4 minutes more. Brush with the glaze and continue to cook until the chops reach an internal temperature of 145°F (63°C), 5 to 6 minutes.

Remove the glazed chops from the grill and let them rest for about 10 minutes before serving.

Skirt Steak Fajitas

Makes 4 servings

My favorite dish at Mariachi Restaurant in Rehoboth Beach, Delaware, is the steak fajitas. This Tex-Mex classic features a boldly flavored fajita marinade that both seasons and tenderizes the meat. To replicate the smoky char of the restaurant's grill, cook the steak quickly over high heat in the EGG. Here is my version.

MARINADE

½ cup (120 ml) fresh orange juice

¼ cup (60 ml) fresh lime juice

¼ cup (60 ml) soy sauce

2 tbsp (30 ml) olive oil

½ tsp chili powder

1 tsp ground cumin

½ tsp smoked paprika

½ tsp salt

½ tsp freshly ground black pepper

⅛ tsp cayenne pepper

2 tbsp (5 g) chopped fresh cilantro

2 tbsp (20 g) minced garlic

1½ lb (680 g) skirt steak, cut into 3 equal portions

4 bell peppers, assorted colors, seeded and sliced into thin strips

1 large onion, sliced

TO SERVE

Sliced limes

12 flour tortillas, warmed

Optional fixings: sliced avocado, pico de gallo, shredded cheese, sour cream

Marinate the steak: In a large bowl, whisk together the marinade ingredients. Place the skirt steak in a large ziplock bag and pour in three-quarters of the marinade to cover the meat. Place the bell peppers and onion in another ziplock bag and pour in the remaining one-quarter of the marinade. Seal up both bags and place them in the refrigerator to marinate for about 4 hours.

Set up the EGG for 450°F (230°C) direct grilling. Fill your firebox with natural lump charcoal, and with the top and bottom vents wide open, light the fire and close the EGG. After about 10 minutes, close the bottom draft screen. When the temperature nears your 450°F (230°C) target temperature, partially close the bottom vent door and the top of the daisy wheel, leaving both vents 50 percent open. Make minor adjustments as necessary.

Once the EGG comes up to temperature, remove the meat from the marinade and discard the marinade. Place the steak on one side of the cooking grid and cook for 3 to 4 minutes. Flip the steak and continue to cook until it reaches an internal temperature of 120°F (49°C) for medium rare, 2 to 3 minutes, or until your desired doneness. Transfer the steak to a cutting board and allow it to rest for about 10 minutes. Slice the meat against the grain into thin strips and set aside.

While the steak is cooking, place a 12-inch (30-cm) cast-iron skillet on the other side of the cooking grid and allow it to heat up. Transfer the bell peppers and onion to the hot skillet and discard the marinade. Sauté the peppers and onion until they begin to soften, about 3 minutes. Close the lid and continue to cook until tender, 3 to 4 minutes longer.

To serve, arrange the sliced steak, peppers, onion, cut limes and warmed tortillas on a platter. Serve with your desired toppings.

Oklahoma Onion Burgers

Makes 4 servings

The delicious pairing of beef and onions in this Oklahoma state classic has withstood the test of time. In fact, it is one of America's great regional burger styles. Thinly sliced sweet onion is smashed into a beef patty on a hot cast-iron skillet, resulting in a golden caramelized onion that is embedded in a perfectly cooked, juicy burger with a crispy crust.

Grapeseed oil

1½ lb (680 g) 80/20 ground chuck, rolled into 8 (3-oz [85-g]) balls

Kosher salt

Freshly ground black pepper

1 large, sweet onion, sliced extra thin

8 slices American cheese, such as Cooper Sharp

4 potato rolls, such as Martin's, split and toasted

Prepared yellow mustard, ketchup and pickles, for serving

Set up the EGG for 400°F (200°C) direct grilling. Fill your firebox with natural lump charcoal, and with the top and bottom vents wide open, light the fire and close the EGG. After about 10 minutes, close the bottom draft screen. When the temperature nears your 400°F (200°C) target temperature, partially close the bottom vent door and the top of the daisy wheel, leaving both vents 40 percent open. Make minor adjustments as necessary.

Place a large, cast-iron skillet on the cooking grid to preheat for about 20 minutes. Drizzle 1 tablespoon (15 ml) of oil into the skillet and, using the flat side of your spatula, spread it around to coat the surface of the pan.

Place two of the meatballs in the hot pan. Close the lid and allow them to sear for 30 seconds. Season the meat with salt and pepper and top each burger with a small handful of the onion slices, pressing them down in the center to adhere to the meat. Using a heavy-duty metal spatula, press the balls down to flatten until they are about ¼ inch (6 mm) thick. With the lid open, cook the burgers for 2 minutes. Flip the patties, close the lid and continue to cook for 2 minutes more. Top each burger with a slice of cheese, close the lid and cook for 1 minute, or until the cheese is melted. Transfer the burgers to a sheet pan and tent loosely with foil to keep warm. Working in batches, continue to cook the remaining burgers.

To build your burger, spread the bottom half of each bun with mustard and ketchup. Then, stack two burger patties with their cheese and onion. Top each burger with a few pickle slices and the top bun.

ASIAN-STYLE PORK BURGERS
with CRUNCHY SLAW AND YUM YUM SAUCE

Makes 4 servings

If you are in the mood for a thick, juicy burger but want something a bit different, give these flavor-packed Asian-style burgers a try. Top them off with crunchy slaw and a Japanese hibachi–inspired sauce for a savory, sweet and tangy bite.

CRUNCHY SLAW

2 tsp (10 ml) rice vinegar

1 tsp soy sauce

2 tsp (10 ml) olive oil

1 tsp fresh lime juice

1 (1-lb [455-g]) package coleslaw mix

1 tbsp (2 g) thinly sliced scallion

YUM YUM SAUCE

1¼ cups (281 g) mayonnaise

2 tbsp (32 g) tomato paste

1 tbsp (15 ml) rice vinegar

1 tsp paprika

1 tsp garlic powder

1 tbsp (13 g) sugar

1 tbsp (15 ml) melted butter

Salt and black pepper

2 tbsp (30 ml) water

BURGERS

1½ lb (680 g) ground pork

1 tbsp (7 g) finely grated fresh ginger

1 tbsp (3 g) thinly sliced scallion

2 tsp (6 g) minced garlic

1¼ tsp (6 ml) sesame oil

2 tsp (12 g) kosher salt

½ tsp freshly ground black pepper

4 hamburger buns, split and toasted

Prepare the slaw: In a medium-sized bowl, combine the vinegar, soy sauce, olive oil and lime juice. Add the coleslaw and scallion and mix well. Refrigerate the slaw until ready to use.

Prepare the sauce: In a medium-sized bowl, whisk together the mayonnaise, tomato paste, vinegar, paprika, garlic powder, sugar and melted butter. Season to taste with salt and pepper. Adjust to your desired consistency with water, adding 1 tablespoon (15 ml) at a time. Refrigerate the sauce until ready to use.

Prepare the burger patties: In a large bowl, combine the pork, ginger, scallion, garlic, sesame oil, salt and pepper. Divide the pork mixture into four equal portions, shaping each into a 1-inch (2.5-cm)-thick patty. Refrigerate them for 30 minutes, or until you're ready to cook.

Set up the EGG for 400°F (200°C) direct grilling. Fill your firebox with natural lump charcoal, and with the top and bottom vents wide open, light the fire and close the EGG. After about 10 minutes, close the bottom draft screen. When the temperature nears your 400°F (200°C) target temperature, partially close the bottom vent door and the top of the daisy wheel, leaving both vents 40 percent open. Make minor adjustments as necessary.

Place the patties directly on the grid and cook for 5 to 6 minutes. Flip the burgers and continue to cook until they reach an internal temperature of 160°F (71°C), 5 to 6 minutes.

Transfer the cooked burgers to a plate and tent them with foil to rest.

To build each burger, layer the bottom half of each bun with the sauce, a burger patty and crunchy slaw. Then, add a toasted bun top.

Spicy Jerk Shrimp Cocktail
with Cool Island Dipping Sauce

Makes 4 to 6 servings

Shrimp cocktail always seems to be a crowd-pleaser, and this one is no different. These Caribbean-style shrimp are full of aromatic spices, thanks to the homemade jerk seasoning. If you can't take the heat, don't worry; the dipping sauce is a great counter and complement to the spice. You can serve the shrimp hot from the grill, or if you prefer, allow them to cool and serve chilled.

JERK SEASONING RUB

2 tbsp (15 g) granulated garlic

2 tbsp (16 g) onion powder

2 tbsp (30 g) light brown sugar

2 tbsp (3 g) dried parsley

1 tbsp (7 g) smoked paprika

1 tbsp (19 g) kosher salt

1 tbsp (3 g) dried thyme

1 tbsp (5 g) cayenne pepper

1½ tsp (1 g) ground allspice

1½ tsp (3 g) ground black pepper

1 tsp ground cumin

1 tsp freshly grated nutmeg

1 tsp ground cinnamon

ISLAND DIPPING SAUCE

⅔ cup (120 ml) ketchup

½ cup (115 g) mayonnaise

2 tbsp (30 g) prepared horseradish

2 tsp (10 ml) fresh lemon juice

1 lb (455 g) jumbo shrimp (16–20 count), peeled and deveined, tail on

2 tsp (10 ml) olive oil

Prepare the rub: In a medium-sized bowl, stir together all the rub ingredients, then set aside. Leftover rub may be stored in an airtight container for up to 6 months.

Prepare the dipping sauce: In a small bowl, stir together the ketchup, mayonnaise, horseradish and lemon juice. Cover and refrigerate until ready to serve.

Set up the EGG for 350°F (180°C) direct grilling. Fill your firebox with natural lump charcoal, and with the top and bottom vents wide open, light the fire and close the EGG. After about 10 minutes, close the bottom draft screen. When the temperature nears your 350°F (180°C) target temperature, partially close the bottom vent door and the top of the daisy wheel, leaving both vents 30 percent open. Make minor adjustments as necessary.

In a medium-sized bowl, toss the shrimp to coat with olive oil and season with an even coating of the jerk rub. Once the cooker comes up to temperature, place the shrimp on the cooking grid and grill over direct heat until they are firm to the touch and just turning opaque in the center, 3 to 4 minutes per side.

Remove the shrimp from the grill and arrange on a platter. Serve with the dipping sauce on the side.

Seared Scallops over Warm Corn Salad

Makes 2 servings

This is a quick and delicious meal that pays homage to the classic pairing of scallops and bacon. Start by searing the scallops in a hot cast-iron pan on the EGG to form a golden-brown crust, then set them atop the summer's bounty of sweet corn and bell peppers. Sprinkle the finished dish with crumbled bacon for an irresistible smoky and crunchy bite.

SCALLOPS

1 lb (455 g) U10 dry sea scallops

Kosher salt

Freshly ground black pepper

2 tbsp (30 ml) olive oil

CORN SALAD

1 tbsp (15 ml) olive oil

1 red bell pepper, seeded and diced

2 tbsp (5 g) thinly sliced scallion

1 small shallot, diced

1 jalapeño pepper, seeded and diced

1 tbsp (10 g) minced garlic

2 cups (300 g) corn kernels, cut from 3 large ears

Kosher salt

Freshly ground black pepper

4 slices bacon, cooked and crumbled, for serving

Set up the EGG for 400°F (200°C) direct grilling. Fill your firebox with natural lump charcoal, and with the top and bottom vents wide open, light the fire and close the EGG. After about 10 minutes, close the bottom draft screen. When the temperature nears your 400°F (200°C) target temperature, partially close the bottom vent door and the top of the daisy wheel, leaving both vents 40 percent open. Make minor adjustments as necessary.

Place a 12-inch (30-cm) cast-iron skillet on the cooking grid to preheat for about 20 minutes.

Prepare the scallops: Peel away the side muscle, a.k.a. the foot, from the scallops and pat dry. Season both sides of the scallops with salt and black pepper and refrigerate until ready to cook. Heat the oil until it shimmers in the skillet, then place the scallops in the pan and cook until they are golden brown on one side, about 2 minutes. Flip the scallops and cook until they are firm to the touch but still slightly soft, 1 to 2 minutes. Using a pair of tongs, transfer the scallops to a platter and loosely tent with foil, leaving the pan on the cooking grid.

Prepare the corn salad: Heat the oil in the cast-iron skillet and add the bell pepper, scallion, shallot, jalapeño and garlic. Cook for 3 to 4 minutes, or until the vegetables are slightly tender. Add the corn and cook for an additional 2 minutes, or until warmed through. Season with salt and black pepper to taste.

To serve: Spoon the corn salad onto plates and top with the scallops and bacon.

LOBSTER TAILS *with* HERB GARLIC BUTTER

Makes 4 servings

I used to own a fresh fish market on the Jersey shore. The question customers asked the most was "How do you cook it?" Most seafood is quick and easy to prepare, and these grilled lobster tails are no exception. Simple yet elegant, lobster tails are the type of indulgence that doesn't need much added to it. In this case, however, quickly charring the lobster meat over hot coals before brushing with the addictive herb garlic butter elevates this dish to five-star status.

HERB GARLIC BUTTER

½ cup (112 g/1 stick) unsalted butter, at room temperature

1 tbsp (4 g) finely chopped fresh parsley

1 tbsp (4 g) finely chopped tarragon leaves

1 tbsp (3 g) finely chopped fresh chives

2 tbsp (20 g) minced garlic

½ tsp kosher salt

1 tsp lemon zest

1 tsp fresh lemon juice

4 (5- to 6-oz [140- to 170-g]) lobster tails

Extra-virgin olive oil

Kosher salt

Freshly ground black pepper

Prepare the herb garlic butter: In a medium-sized bowl, combine the butter, parsley, tarragon, chives, garlic, salt, lemon zest and lemon juice. Using a spoon or silicone spatula, place the butter mixture on a piece of plastic wrap and roll it into the shape of a log. Twist the ends to seal, then refrigerate for 1 hour, or until ready to use.

Set up the EGG for 450°F (230°C) direct grilling. Fill your firebox with natural lump charcoal, and with the top and bottom vents wide open, light the fire and close the EGG. After about 10 minutes, close the bottom draft screen. When the temperature nears your 450°F (230°C) target temperature, partially close the bottom vent door and the top of the daisy wheel, leaving both vents 50 percent open. Make minor adjustments as necessary.

Prepare the lobster tails: Using kitchen shears, cut the top of the lobster shell from the meaty portion of the tail. Using a knife, cut the lobster tail in half lengthwise through the meat down the center. Brush the lobster meat with the olive oil and season with salt and pepper. Once the EGG comes up to temperature, place the lobster tails, cut side down, on the grid and cook until the lobster meat is lightly charred, 2 to 3 minutes. Flip the tails, close the lid and continue to cook until they reach an internal temperature of 140°F (60°C), about 5 minutes. Transfer the tails to a disposable aluminum half pan and top each tail with 1½ teaspoons (7 g) of the herb garlic butter. Place the pan on the grill and close the lid to melt the butter, 1 to 2 minutes. Arrange the tails on a platter and brush them with melted butter from the pan. Serve immediately.

Seared Ahi Tuna
with Lemon Caper Vinaigrette
Makes 2 servings

When you're craving a lean, meaty protein, these seared tuna steaks are the perfect choice. The salty, briny capers punch up the flavor in the vinaigrette while the acidity of the lemon works to balance it against the mild tuna.

LEMON CAPER VINAIGRETTE

½ cup (65 g) packed fresh parsley leaves

½ cup (120 ml) extra-virgin olive oil

3 tbsp (45 ml) white wine vinegar

3 tbsp (45 ml) fresh lemon juice

½ tsp minced garlic

1 tsp Dijon mustard

1 tsp honey

2 tbsp (17 g) capers

¼ tsp freshly ground black pepper

2 tbsp (16 g) white sesame seeds

2 tbsp (16 g) black sesame seeds

2 (5- to 6-oz [140- to 170-g]) thick-cut ahi tuna steaks

Olive oil

Kosher salt

Freshly ground black pepper

Prepare the vinaigrette: In a blender, puree the parsley, oil, vinegar, lemon juice, garlic, mustard, honey, capers and pepper until the parsley is finely chopped and the mixture thickens slightly. Transfer to a glass jar and set aside.

In a small bowl, combine the white and black sesame seeds, then set it aside.

Set up the EGG for 400°F (200°C) direct grilling. Fill your firebox with natural lump charcoal, and with the top and bottom vents wide open, light the fire and close the EGG. After about 10 minutes, close the bottom draft screen. When the temperature nears your 400°F (200°C) target temperature, partially close the bottom vent door and the top of the daisy wheel, leaving both vents 40 percent open. Make minor adjustments as necessary.

Place a 12-inch (30-cm) cast-iron skillet on the cooking grid to preheat for about 20 minutes. While the pan is heating, brush the steaks with olive oil and season them with salt and pepper. Spread out the sesame seeds on a plate and press the steaks into the seeds to coat on both sides. Refrigerate the tuna until ready to cook. Once the pan is hot, drizzle in some olive oil and place the steaks in the skillet. Cook with the lid open for 1½ minutes. Flip the steaks and continue to cook for 1½ minutes more for rare. The cooking times may vary according to your preferred level of doneness. By inspecting the side of the fish as it cooks, you can visually gauge how fast it is cooking. Using a pair of metal tongs or a spatula, transfer the fish to a plate and allow it to rest for a few minutes. Drizzle the steaks with the lemon caper vinaigrette to serve.

Blackened Salmon *with* Pineapple Salsa

Makes 4 servings

My family loves salmon, and we are always on the hunt for simple and flavorful ways to prepare it. Searing the fillets quickly over high heat in the EGG, rather than cooking them at a lower temperature for a longer period of time, not only ensures a well-developed crust, it also helps prevent the salmon from drying out. The sweetness of the pineapple salsa is a great counterpoint to the spicy fish.

BLACKENING SPICE RUB

3 tbsp (21 g) paprika

2 tbsp (5 g) dried thyme

2 tsp (5 g) onion powder

2 tsp (6 g) garlic powder

2 tsp (2 g) dried oregano

2 tsp (2 g) sea salt

2 tsp (4 g) freshly ground black pepper

2 tsp (4 g) cayenne pepper

PINEAPPLE SALSA

1 large pineapple peeled, cored and diced

1 jalapeño pepper, seeds and ribs removed, finely diced

½ cup (80 g) diced sweet onion

3 tbsp (45 ml) fresh lime juice

3 tbsp (8 g) chopped fresh cilantro

Kosher salt

Freshly ground black pepper

4 (6-oz [170-g]) salmon fillets, skin on

2 tbsp (30 ml) olive oil

Prepare the spice rub: In a medium-sized bowl, stir together all the rub ingredients, then set aside. Leftover rub may be stored in an airtight container for up to 6 months.

Prepare the salsa: In a medium-sized bowl, combine the pineapple, jalapeño, onion, lime juice, cilantro and salt and black pepper to taste. Cover and refrigerate until ready to serve.

Set up the EGG for 400°F (200°C) direct grilling. Fill your firebox with natural lump charcoal, and with the top and bottom vents wide open, light the fire and close the EGG. After about 10 minutes, close the bottom draft screen. When the temperature nears your 400°F (200°C) target temperature, partially close the bottom vent door and the top of the daisy wheel, leaving both vents 40 percent open. Make minor adjustments as necessary.

Place a large, cast-iron skillet on the cooking grid to preheat for about 20 minutes. Season both sides of the salmon fillets with an even coating of the blackening spice. Heat the oil until it shimmers in the skillet. Place the fillets in the pan, skin side up, and cook for 3 to 4 minutes. Using a pair of metal tongs or a spatula, flip the fish and continue to cook until it reaches an internal temperature of 145°F (63°C), 5 to 6 minutes, depending on the thickness of your fillets. Arrange the salmon on a platter with the pineapple salsa to serve.

Award-Winning Maryland-Style Crab Cakes

Makes 4 to 6 servings

Have you ever thought about frying crab cakes on your grill? The Big Green Egg can do it. After all, it's the most versatile cooking appliance on the market today. The benefit to cooking these crab cakes outside is that you won't heat up your house or stink it up for days, I recommend using a high-sided Dutch oven while frying over a live fire, to avoid splattering oil onto the hot coals below. This recipe was awarded First Place and the title of "Delaware's Best Crab Cake" at the 30th annual Coast Day Crab Cake Cook-off, held in Lewes, Delaware.

1 large egg

½ cup (115 g) mayonnaise

1 tbsp (11 g) Dijon mustard

2 tsp (5 g) Old Bay seasoning

2 tbsp (30 ml) fresh lemon juice

1 tsp hot sauce

Kosher salt

Freshly ground black pepper

¼ cup (45 g) minced red onion

2 tbsp (4 g) thinly sliced scallion

¼ cup (30 g) minced celery

½ cup (60 g) unseasoned dried bread crumbs

1 tbsp (4 g) chopped fresh tarragon

⅓ cup (38 g) shredded sharp Cheddar cheese

⅓ cup (38 g) shredded pepper Jack cheese

1 lb (455 g) lump crabmeat, picked over, shells and cartilage removed

2 cups (120 g) unseasoned panko bread crumbs, for coating crab cakes

1 cup (240 ml) heavy cream

Vegetable oil, for frying

Store-bought rémoulade sauce and lemon wedges, for serving

Set up the EGG for 400°F (200°C) direct grilling. Fill your firebox with natural lump charcoal, and with the top and bottom vents wide open, light the fire and close the EGG. After about 10 minutes, close the bottom draft screen. When the temperature nears your 400°F (200°C) target temperature, partially close the bottom vent door and the top of the daisy wheel, leaving both vents 40 percent open. Make minor adjustments as necessary.

In a large bowl, whisk together the egg, mayonnaise, mustard, Old Bay seasoning, lemon juice, hot sauce and a generous pinch of salt and pepper. Add the red onion, scallion, celery, bread crumbs, tarragon, shredded Cheddar and pepper Jack cheeses and crabmeat; mix gently until well combined, taking care not to overmix. Form the crab mixture into about 12 cakes. Spread the panko on a plate. One at a time, dip the cakes into the heavy cream, and then coat them with the panko. Place the crab cakes on a sheet pan and refrigerate them until you are ready to cook.

Pour the oil into a Dutch oven until about 2 inches (5 cm) deep. Cover and place the Dutch oven on the cooking grate and close the lid. Heat the EGG until the oil reaches 375°F (190°C). Do not close the lid unless the cover is on the Dutch oven. If the oil gets too hot, cover the Dutch oven, take it off the EGG and allow it to cool before proceeding.

Fry the crab cakes in batches, 3 or 4 at a time (don't overcrowd the pan; it will bring the temperature of the oil down) for 2 to 3 minutes. Using a pair of metal tongs, gently flip the crab cakes over and continue to cook until they reach an internal temperature of 155°F (68°C) and are golden brown, about 2 minutes. Carefully transfer the crab cakes from the hot oil to a paper towel–lined sheet pan to drain. Allow them to cool for 1 to 2 minutes.

Arrange the crab cakes on a platter with rémoulade sauce and lemon wedges to serve.

Cajun Char-Grilled Oysters

Makes 2 servings

When these garlicky oysters come off the grill, they'll be oozing with butter and cheese. Make sure you have some crusty bread for sopping up all the juices.

12 oysters

½ cup (112 g/1 stick) unsalted butter, at room temperature

2 tsp (6 g) minced garlic

2 tbsp (30 ml) fresh) lemon juice

1 tsp Worcestershire sauce

¾ cup (75 g) grated Pecorino Romano or Parmesan cheese, divided

1 tbsp (4 g) chopped fresh parsley, plus 2 tbsp (8 g) for serving

Kosher salt

Freshly ground black pepper

Cayenne pepper

Place the oysters in a colander and rinse under cold running water. Use a scrub brush to remove any mud or debris, if necessary. Refrigerate the oysters with the cup side down and their flat side facing up. Cover with a clean, wet kitchen towel until ready to cook.

Prepare the Cajun butter: In a medium-sized bowl combine the butter, garlic, lemon juice, Worcestershire sauce, ¼ cup (25 g) of the cheese, parsley, salt, black pepper and cayenne to taste. Using a spoon or silicone spatula, place the butter mixture onto a piece of plastic wrap and roll it into the shape of a log. Twist the ends to seal, then refrigerate for 1 hour, or until ready to use.

Set up the EGG for 450°F (230°C) direct grilling. Fill your firebox with natural lump charcoal, and with the top and bottom vents wide open, light the fire and close the EGG. After about 10 minutes, close the bottom draft screen. When the temperature nears your 450°F (230°C) target temperature, partially close the bottom vent door and the top of the daisy wheel, leaving both vents 50 percent open. Make minor adjustments as necessary.

Shuck the oysters: Set an oyster on a flat working surface with the flatter side facing up. Use a kitchen towel to hold it steady, and with your other hand, slide the tip of an oyster knife into the hinge. Press the knife into the hinge and twist the blade to pop it open. Slide the knife between the shells, keeping it along the bottom of the top shell and then along the bottom shell to release the oyster meat. This will make it easier to eat after it is done cooking. Keep the oyster as flat as possible while working, to avoid spilling out the oyster liquor inside.

Place the oysters, in their half shells, on the cooking grid over the hot coals. Cook until the oysters begin to bubble in their shells, 2 to 3 minutes. Spoon 2 teaspoons (10 g) of the butter mixture onto each oyster and top with a sprinkle of the remaining cheese. Close the lid and continue to cook until the cheese is beginning to brown, 3 to 4 minutes. Arrange the oysters on a platter to serve.

Rack of Lamb
with Parsley and Mint Gremolata
Makes 4 servings

Once grilled, this tender rack of lamb is carved into juicy chops and accompanied by an herbaceous and refreshing mint-infused gremolata.

TEMPERATURE DONENESS GUIDE FOR LAMB

- Rare 125°F (52°C)
- Medium Rare 135°F (57°C)
- Medium 145°F (63°C)
- Medium Well 155°F (68°C)
- Well Done 165°F (73°C)

LAMB CHOPS

1 (8-bone) lamb rib rack, trimmed and frenched (fat and meat removed from the bones to create a handle)

¼ cup (60 ml) olive oil

4 or 5 sprigs mint, chopped

2 tsp (6 g) chopped garlic

Kosher salt

Freshly ground black pepper

1 lemon, sliced and grilled, for serving (optional)

PARSLEY AND MINT GREMOLATA

1 tsp chopped garlic

¼ tsp lemon zest

2 tsp (10 ml) fresh lemon juice

⅛ tsp kosher salt

½ cup (30 g) flat-leaf parsley, finely chopped

¼ cup (10 g) loosely packed fresh mint leaves, finely chopped

1 tbsp (15 ml) olive oil

Marinate the lamb: Place the lamb rack, olive oil, mint and garlic in a large, resealable plastic bag. Toss to coat the lamb and marinate in the refrigerator for 2 to 3 hours.

Prepare the gremolata: In a small bowl, stir together the garlic, lemon zest, lemon juice, salt, parsley, mint and olive oil. Cover and refrigerate until ready to serve.

Set up the EGG for 450°F (230°C) direct grilling. Fill your firebox with natural lump charcoal, and with the top and bottom vents wide open, light the fire and close the EGG. After about 10 minutes, close the bottom draft screen. When the temperature nears your 450°F (230°C) target temperature, partially close the bottom vent door and the top of the daisy wheel, leaving both vents 50 percent open. Make minor adjustments as necessary.

Prepare the lamb: Remove the lamb rack from the marinade and discard the marinade. Pat the meat dry and season with salt and pepper. Wrap the top of the bones with foil to protect them from getting charred or burnt as the meat cooks. If you are not overly concerned with the darkening of the bones, skip this step. It is for presentation and will not affect the flavor of your meat. When the EGG comes up to temperature, place the lamb rack, meat side down, directly on the cooking grid to sear for 5 to 6 minutes. Turn the lamb over and continue to cook until it reaches an internal temperature of 135°F (57°C) for medium rare, 10 to 12 minutes. Remove the lamb from the grill and allow it to rest for about 10 minutes. Using a carving knife, cut the meat between the bones to make chops. Transfer the chops to a serving platter and garnish with the gremolata and grilled lemon (if using) to serve.

COLLARD GREENS *with* BEANS AND BACON

Makes about 6 servings

This hearty southern-style side dish has been a fan favorite on my pop-up menus for some time. It pairs well with barbecued meats, and it is great on its own over rice.

5 slices thick-cut bacon, sliced crosswise into 1" (2.5-cm) pieces, divided

1 large onion, diced

2 tbsp (20 g) minced garlic

1 (14.5-oz [429-ml]) can low-sodium chicken stock

2 (1-lb [455-g]) bags precut and washed collard greens

Kosher salt

Freshly ground black pepper

2 (15-oz [425-g]) cans red kidney beans, drained and rinsed

¼ tsp crushed red pepper flakes

Set up the EGG for 400°F (200°C) direct grilling. Fill your firebox with natural lump charcoal, and with the top and bottom vents wide open, light the fire and close the EGG. After about 10 minutes, close the bottom draft screen. When the temperature nears your 400°F (200°C) target temperature, partially close the bottom vent door and the top of the daisy wheel, leaving both vents 40 percent open. Make minor adjustments as necessary.

Heat a 6-quart (5.7-L) Dutch oven on the grill for about 20 minutes. Once the pan is hot, add one-quarter of the bacon and cook until it is browned and crisp, about 5 minutes. Transfer the bacon to a paper towel–lined plate and set aside. Add the remaining bacon to the pan and cook it just until it starts to render, about 2 minutes. Add the onion and continue to cook, stirring frequently, until it begins to soften, 3 to 4 minutes. Add the garlic to the pan and cook, stirring, until fragrant, about 1 minute. Stir in the stock, close the lid and bring to a simmer, about 5 minutes. Add the greens and season the mixture with salt and pepper to taste. Close the lid and continue to cook until the collards are tender, about 5 minutes. Stir in the beans and crushed red pepper flakes. Cook until the beans are heated through, about 5 minutes. Spoon the collards onto serving dishes and top with the reserved bacon.

Low 'n' Slow
SMOKING, BARBECUE

If you would like to barbecue the most succulent cuts of meat the way they were meant to be eaten, then this low and slow cooking technique is for you. By definition, the word *barbecue* means to use charcoal or wood to cook meat over a low heat source for a long period of time. The food is cooked indirectly, with temperatures that generally range from 225 to 275°F (110 to 140°C). This method is great for larger, tougher cuts of meat. The long, slow cooking process helps render the fat and break down connective tissue, yielding a tender, smoky bite.

Meat, smoking wood and time are all essential ingredients, but the key to cooking low and slow on the Big Green Egg is to manage the airflow. One way to do this is to use quality lump charcoal, which produces less ash. Having less ash in your firebox means that there is less chance of your air vents getting blocked, cutting off crucial oxygen that is needed to fuel your fire. I recommend cleaning the excess ash out of your firebox regularly. The EGG's thick ceramic walls provide insulation of the cooking chamber and assist in maintaining a steady temperature and moist cooking environment throughout the long cook.

In this chapter, you will learn the secrets to smoking traditional barbecue favorites, such as Pulled Pork with Carolina Mustard BBQ Sauce (page 58), St. Louis–Style Pork Ribs (page 62) and Texas-Style Brisket and Burnt Ends (page 65), as well as some new flavor-packed dishes, such as Mexican Roadside Chicken (page 61), Cherry Chipotle Glazed Ham (page 83) and a Smoked Queso Beer Dip (page 91) that is tailgate ready. Let's get the smoke rolling!

Pulled Pork
with Carolina Mustard BBQ Sauce

Makes about 12 servings

Making pulled pork is a great way to get started with low and slow cooking on your Big Green Egg. Pork butt is the perfect choice because it is a well marbled and flavorful cut of meat that is also very forgiving. Smoke the butt slowly until it is pull-apart tender, then drizzle the meat with the sweet and tangy golden sauce.

CAROLINA MUSTARD BBQ SAUCE

1 cup (176 g) prepared yellow mustard

½ cup (120 ml) cider vinegar

¼ cup (60 ml) honey

¼ cup (60 g) packed light brown sugar

2 tsp (20 ml) Worcestershire sauce

2 tbsp (30 ml) ketchup

1 tsp garlic powder

1½ tsp (2 g) red pepper flakes

½ tsp salt

1 (8- to 9-lb [3.6- to 4-kg]) bone-in pork butt

¼ cup (44 g) prepared yellow mustard

Sweet and Smoky BBQ Rub (page 110)

1 cup (240 ml) apple juice, plus more for spritzing

Prepare the BBQ sauce: In a medium-sized saucepan, combine all the sauce ingredients and heat over medium-low heat, stirring to dissolve the sugar. Lower the heat to low and simmer until slightly thickened, 5 to 7 minutes, stirring frequently. Remove from the heat, let cool, transfer to a jar and store in the refrigerator until ready to use. It will last up to a month.

Trim the pork of any extra or loose hanging fat. Leave the fat cap on, as this helps protect the butt and retain moisture during cooking. Pat the meat dry and rub all over with the mustard. Apply the BBQ rub liberally to the meat. Place the butt in an aluminum half pan. Cover with plastic wrap and refrigerate for at least an hour and up to 8 hours.

Set up the EGG to cook at 275°F (140°C), indirect with a drip pan. Fill your firebox with natural lump charcoal, layering it with four or five chunks of smoking wood. For pork, I like to use a combination of hickory and cherry wood. With the top and bottom vents wide open, light the fire and close the lid. After about 10 minutes, close the bottom draft screen. As the dome temperature approaches your target temperature of 275°F (140°C), about 5 minutes, partially close the bottom vent door and the top of the daisy wheel, leaving both vents 15 percent open. Make minor adjustments as necessary.

Once the EGG reaches temperature, put the butt, fat side down, on the grid in the EGG. Cook until the internal temperature of the pork butt reaches 160 to 170°F (71 to 77°C), about 6 hours, spritzing with apple juice every 30 minutes.

Remove the butt from the EGG. Pour the cup (240 ml) of the apple juice into an aluminum pan and transfer the butt to the pan. Cover the pan with aluminum foil and return it to the EGG. Cook for another 2 to 3 hours, or until the internal temperature reaches 198 to 203°F (92 to 95°C).

Remove the pan from the cooker and open the foil to vent for 10 minutes. This will help to stop the cooking process. Rewrap and place in a dry cooler to rest and stay warm until ready to serve.

When ready to serve: Remove the butt from the cooler and using heavy, insulated gloves, pull the meat apart gently into large chunks. Discard the bone and any fat. Brush the chunks with a light coating of the BBQ sauce and set aside. Shred or pull the remaining meat with your hands. Serve with additional BBQ sauce on the side.

MEXICAN ROADSIDE CHICKEN

Makes 4 servings

This smoke-roasted chicken is infused with the flavors of Mexico and can make those roadside stands feel much closer than they are. Apply the vibrant chile and spice paste a couple of hours before cooking, to ensure that every bite is packed with flavor.

1 (4- to 5-lb [1.8- to 2.5-kg]) chicken

OAXACAN SPICE PASTE

2 tbsp (15 g) ancho chile powder

2 tsp (5 g) chipotle chile powder

1 tsp dried oregano

1 tsp ground cumin

⅛ tsp ground cinnamon

1 tsp ground coriander

½ tsp ground cloves

¼ cup (60 ml) fresh orange juice

3 tbsp (45 ml) cider vinegar

1 tbsp (10 g) minced garlic

1 tsp kosher salt

½ tsp freshly ground black pepper

Lime wedges, to serve

Spatchcock the chicken: Set the chicken on a cutting board, breast side down, with the neck facing toward you. Remove the neck and giblets and pat the chicken dry with paper towels. Using kitchen shears, cut along one side of the backbone, then cut along the other side to remove it. Flip the chicken over, and using the palm of your hands, press hard along the breastbone to flatten the chicken completely. Refrigerate the chicken until ready to use.

In a medium-sized bowl, stir together all the paste ingredients. Using your hands, smear the spice mixture all over the chicken, even tucking it under the skin. You may want to put on a pair of food-safe disposable gloves, as this step can be messy. Transfer the chicken to a sheet pan and cover with plastic wrap. Refrigerate for 2 hours to allow the flavors to develop in the meat.

Set up the EGG for 350°F (180°C), indirect with a drip pan. Fill your firebox with natural lump charcoal, layering it with two chunks of smoking wood. For this dish, I like to use hickory or mesquite wood. With the top and bottom vents wide open, light the fire and close the EGG. After about 10 minutes, close the bottom draft screen. When the temperature nears your 350°F (180°C) target temperature, partially close the bottom vent door and the top of the daisy wheel, leaving both vents 30 percent open. Make minor adjustments as necessary.

Once the cooker comes up to temperature, place the chicken, breast side up, on the cooking grid and close the lid. Cook until the chicken reaches an internal temperature of 180°F (82°C) in the thickest part of the thigh and 165°F (73°C) in the breast, 65 to 75 minutes. Remove the chicken from the grill and allow it to rest for 15 minutes before carving. Serve with lime wedges.

St. Louis–Style Pork Ribs

Makes about 8 servings

What is the first thing that comes to mind when you think about cooking barbecue? How to prepare tender, smoky, flavorful ribs, of course! Here is the recipe that has resulted in numerous top ten calls for our BBQ Buddha competition team.

2 slabs St. Louis–cut pork ribs, about 2½ lb (1.1 kg) each

¼ cup (44 g) prepared yellow mustard

½ cup (120 g) Sweet and Smoky BBQ Rub (page 110), plus more as needed

Apple juice, for spritzing

½ cup (120 ml) honey

1 cup (225 g) packed light brown sugar

¼ cup (60 ml) hot sauce, such as Crystal brand

¼ cup (55 g/½ stick) unsalted butter, melted

1 cup (240 ml) Kansas City BBQ Sauce (page 88), warmed

Set up the EGG for 250°F (120°C), indirect with a drip pan. Fill your firebox with natural lump charcoal, layering it with three or four chunks of smoking wood. A combination of hickory and cherry wood will pair well with these ribs. With the top and bottom vents wide open, light the fire and close the EGG. After about 10 minutes, close the bottom draft screen. When the temperature nears your 250°F (120°C) target temperature, partially close the bottom vent door and the top of the daisy wheel, leaving both vents 10 percent open. Make minor adjustments as necessary.

Remove the membrane from the back of the ribs and trim any excess fat. Remove the end bones from each slab to square them up. Apply a thin coat of mustard to each side. Sprinkle on an even layer of the BBQ rub to both sides of the ribs. Let them sit for 30 minutes to let the rub set up.

Once the EGG reaches temperature, place the ribs on the grid and cook for 2½ hours, spritzing with apple juice every 30 minutes. Lay out two sheets of heavy-duty aluminum foil. Layer half of the honey, brown sugar, hot sauce and butter on each sheet of the foil. Lightly dust with some more of the rub and spritz with apple juice. Place a slab of the ribs, meat side down, on the mixture and wrap up the foil packages tightly. Place the wrapped ribs back on the smoker and close the lid. Continue to cook for about an hour, then check the ribs for doneness by opening the packages and pushing a toothpick into the meat. It should go in and out easily. Continue to cook to your desired tenderness. Once the ribs are done, remove them from the EGG and open the foil to vent for about 10 minutes. This will prevent the ribs from further cooking.

Brush both sides of the ribs with the warmed BBQ sauce and place back on the smoker to set the glaze, 15 to 20 minutes. Remove ribs from the cooker and allow to rest for 5 minutes. Slice the ribs individually and arrange on a platter to serve.

Texas-Style Brisket and Burnt Ends

Makes about 8 to 10 servings

In Texas, a melt-in-your-mouth brisket with a smoky and peppery crust is king. Burnt ends, however, are a standard of quality in Kansas City barbecue. This recipe gives you the best technique of both barbecue regions. A whole packer brisket is simply seasoned with salt and pepper (a.k.a. Dalmatian rub), before being slow smoked for hours to break down the connective tissues in the meat. After cooking, the point (fatty) end of the brisket is cubed and tossed with BBQ sauce and cooked again to render fat and give the delicious nuggets of meat candy a sweet and sticky glaze.

1 (12- to 14-lb [5.4- to 6.4-kg]) whole choice grade or higher packer beef brisket

¼ cup (60 ml) olive oil

½ cup (150 g) kosher salt

½ cup (51 g) ground black pepper

1 cup (240 ml) Kansas City BBQ Sauce (page 88)

Place the brisket, fat side up, on a cutting board and trim the fat down to about ¼ inch (6 mm). Turn the meat over and trim all fat pockets and silver skin from the surface of the meat. Cut away any loose or gray edges to retain its shape and appearance.

Place the brisket in a large disposable aluminum pan and rub all over with the olive oil. Sprinkle the salt and pepper evenly over the meat and press firmly with your hand to adhere the spices.

Cover and refrigerate the brisket for at least 4 hours and up to overnight.

Set up the EGG for 275°F (140°C), indirect with a drip pan. Fill your firebox with natural lump charcoal, layering it with four or five chunks of smoking wood. For brisket, I like to use oak or hickory wood. With the top and bottom vents wide open, light the fire and close the EGG. After about 10 minutes, close the bottom draft screen. When the temperature nears your 275°F (140°C) target temperature, partially close the bottom vent door and the top of the daisy wheel, leaving both vents 15 percent open. Make minor adjustments as necessary.

Once the cooker reaches temperature, place the brisket, fat side down, on the cooking grate and close the lid. Cook until the internal temperature of the brisket reaches 165°F (73°C), 4 to 5 hours.

Using heavy insulated gloves, transfer the brisket, with the fat side down, to a double layer of aluminum foil or butcher paper and wrap it up tightly. Place the wrapped brisket back on the smoker and cook until the internal temperature reaches 198 to 203°F (92 to 95°C) and a thermometer pushed into the meat gives little resistance.

(continued)

Remove the brisket from the smoker and open the wrap to vent for 10 to 15 minutes. Strain the accumulated juices of their fat into a bowl and allow it to cool. Refrigerate the jus until ready to use.

Close the foil or butcher paper and wrap the brisket in a clean towel; place in an empty, dry cooler to rest for a minimum of 1 hour.

Place the reserved liquid in a medium-sized saucepan and bring to a simmer over medium heat.

Prepare the burnt ends: Once rested, transfer the brisket to a large cutting board. Separate the flat from the point. This is done by using a large carving knife to slice along the fat that is between the two muscles. Wrap the flat back up and return it to the dry cooler.

Cut the point into 1-inch (2.5-cm) cubes and place the meat in a disposable aluminum half pan. Add ¼ cup (60 ml) of the reserved liquid and the BBQ sauce and place it back on the cooker for 1 hour. Remove the pan from the smoker and gently coat the burnt ends with the sauce, then place it back on the cooker for 15 minutes to set the glaze.

While you are waiting for the burnt ends to finish, slice the brisket against the grain about the thickness of a number 2 pencil (about ¼ inch [6 mm] thick). You can slice it a little thicker if it is overcooked or a little thinner if it is a bit tougher, to get the tenderness just right.

Dip each slice of brisket in the warmed jus and arrange on a platter with the burnt ends to serve.

Smoked Corned Beef Brisket, a.k.a. Pastrami

Makes 6 to 8 servings

This DIY pastrami recipe is a game changer. Beef brisket is brine-cured, then seasoned with a peppery spice blend before being smoked low and slow on the EGG. This recipe takes a little time and planning, but the payoff is an incredibly tender, flavorful cut of meat, similar to what is served in New York–style delicatessens.

PASTRAMI RUB

¼ cup (26 g) coarsely ground black pepper

2 tbsp (12 g) ground coriander

1 tsp dry mustard

1 tbsp (15 g) light brown sugar

1 tbsp (7 g) paprika

2 tsp (6 g) garlic powder

2 tsp (5 g) onion powder

BRINE

1 gal (3.8 L) water

1 cup (300 g) kosher salt

½ cup (115 g) packed light brown sugar

1 tsp Prague powder (pink pickling salt)

6 to 8 cloves garlic, crushed

¼ cup (25 g) pickling spice

4 bay leaves

1 (5-lb [2.3-kg]) brisket flat

Optional fixings: rye bread, sauerkraut, prepared mustard

Prepare the rub: In a small bowl, combine all the rub ingredients, then set aside.

Prepare the brine: In a large stockpot, combine all the brine ingredients. Bring to a simmer over medium-high heat, stirring to dissolve the salt and sugar. Remove the brine from the heat and allow it to cool to room temperature, then place it in the refrigerator to cool to 45°F (7°C) before using.

Place the brisket, fat side up, on a cutting board and trim the fat down to about ⅛ inch (3 mm). Turn the meat over and trim the silver skin from the surface of the meat.

Place the brisket into a large, nonreactive lidded container. Pour the brine over the brisket to submerge it and cover with the lid. Brine the brisket in the refrigerator for 8 to 10 days.

Remove the brisket from the brine and discard the brine. Rinse the brisket under cool running water to remove any excess salt and pickling spices. Pat dry with paper towels.

Season the brisket generously with the pastrami rub, using your hand to adhere the spices.

(continued)

Smoked Corned Beef Brisket, A.K.A. Pastrami (continued)

Set up the EGG for 275°F (140°C), indirect with a drip pan. Fill your firebox with natural lump charcoal, layering it with four or five chunks of smoking wood. For corned beef, I like to use either apple or pecan wood. With the top and bottom vents wide open, light the fire and close the EGG. After about 10 minutes, close the bottom draft screen. When the temperature nears your 275°F (140°C) target temperature, partially close the bottom vent door and the top of the daisy wheel, leaving both vents 15 percent open. Make minor adjustments as necessary.

Once the cooker reaches temperature, place the brisket, fat side down, on the cooking grate and close the lid. Cook until the internal temperature of the brisket reaches 165°F (73°C), 4 to 5 hours.

Using heavy insulated gloves, transfer the brisket, with the fat side down, to a double layer of aluminum foil or butcher paper and wrap it up tightly. Place the wrapped brisket back on the smoker and cook until the internal temperature reaches 198 to 203°F (92 to 95°C) and a thermometer pushed into the meat gives little resistance. Remove the brisket from the smoker and open the wrap to vent for 10 minutes. Close the foil or butcher paper and wrap the brisket in a clean towel; place in an empty, dry cooler to rest for 1 to 2 hours.

Once rested, transfer the corned beef to a large cutting board, and using a long carving knife, slice the meat against the grain about the thickness of a number 2 pencil (about ¼ inch [6 mm] thick). You can slice it a little thicker if it is overcooked or a little thinner if it is a bit tougher, to get the tenderness just right.

Serve with the optional fixings, if desired.

Dry-Rubbed Memphis-Style Ribs

Makes 4 to 6 servings

Perfecting Memphis-style ribs is all about building layers of flavor. Brush the ribs with a vinegar mop that has been infused with dry rub every 30 minutes to give them their tangy flavor and beautiful mahogany color.

MEMPHIS DRY RUB

½ cup (144 g) sea salt

¼ cup (60 g) turbinado sugar

¼ cup (60 g) light brown sugar

3 tbsp (21 g) paprika

1 tbsp (8 g) chili powder

1 tbsp (8 g) onion powder

1 tbsp (9 g) dry mustard

2 tsp (5 g) granulated garlic

2 tsp (2 g) dried thyme

2 tsp (2 g) dried oregano

1 tsp freshly ground black pepper

1 tsp celery salt

1 tsp ground ginger

1 tsp ground coriander

¾ tsp cayenne pepper

MOP SAUCE

½ cup (120 ml) distilled white vinegar

½ cup (120 ml) water

¼ cup (60 ml) ketchup

2 tbsp (21 g) Memphis dry rub

2 slabs baby back ribs, about 2½ lb (1.1 kg) each

¼ cup (44 g) prepared yellow mustard

In a medium-sized bowl, combine all the rub ingredients, then set aside. Leftover rub may be stored in an airtight container for up to 6 months.

Prepare the mop sauce: In a small bowl, stir together all the mop sauce ingredients. Set aside until ready to use.

Set up the EGG for 250°F (120°C), indirect with a drip pan. Fill your firebox with natural lump charcoal, layering it with two chunks of hickory wood and one chunk of cherry wood. With the top and bottom vents wide open, light the fire and close the EGG. After about 10 minutes, close the bottom draft screen. When the temperature nears your 250°F (120°C) target temperature, partially close the bottom vent door and the top of the daisy wheel, leaving both vents 10 percent open. Make minor adjustments as necessary.

Remove the membrane from the back of the ribs and trim any excess fat. Apply a thin coat of mustard to each side and dust with an even layer of the Memphis dry rub. Let the ribs sit for 30 minutes to let the rub set up. Once the EGG reaches temperature, place the ribs, meat side up, on the cooking grid. Cook for about 5 hours, during which, after 1½ hours, begin brushing with the mop sauce every 30 minutes.

Around the 4-hour mark, start checking the ribs for tenderness by pushing a toothpick into the meat. The ribs are done when a toothpick inserted into the meat goes in and out easily and you can see the meat shrink from the bone by about ¼ inch (6 mm).

Slice the ribs individually and arrange on a platter. Right before serving, give them another glaze of the mop sauce and a light dusting of the dry rub.

Honey Sriracha Glazed Chicken Thighs

Makes 8 servings

If you are looking for a recipe to amp up the flavors of your next cookout, these sweet and spicy chicken thighs are sure to please. This might even be your new favorite way to prepare chicken!

8 chicken thighs
Poultry Brine (page 87)
Kosher salt
Freshly ground black pepper
Granulated garlic

HONEY SRIRACHA GLAZE
¼ cup (60 ml) sriracha
3 tbsp (45 ml) honey
1 tbsp (15 ml) ketchup
1 tbsp (14 g) salted butter
1 tsp fresh lemon juice
2 tsp (10 ml) low-sodium soy sauce

Trim the meat of the thighs and cut away any loose hanging skin or fat to make them all about the same size.

Three hours before you plan to cook, place the chicken thighs into a large, lidded container and pour the brine over the meat. Cover the container and refrigerate for 2 hours.

Remove the chicken thighs from the brine and rinse well. Pat dry with a paper towel and refrigerate them for 1 hour.

Prepare the glaze: In a small saucepan, combine all the glaze ingredients and cook over medium-low heat, stirring to melt the butter. Lower the heat to low and simmer until it's slightly thickened, 3 to 4 minutes, stirring frequently. Keep the glaze warm until ready to use.

Set up the EGG to cook at 275°F (140°C), indirect with a drip pan. Fill your firebox with natural lump charcoal, layering it with two chunks of apple or sugar maple wood. With the top and bottom vents wide open, light the fire and close the lid. After about 10 minutes, close the bottom draft screen. As the dome temperature approaches your target temperature of 275°F (140°C), about 5 minutes, partially close the bottom vent door and the top of the daisy wheel, leaving both vents 15 percent open. Make minor adjustments as necessary.

Once the smoker comes up to temperature, generously season both sides of the chicken with salt, pepper and granulated garlic. Place the thighs, bone side down, directly on the cooking grate, close the lid and cook until the chicken reaches an internal temperature of 165°F (73°C), about 1 hour. Using a silicone brush, baste the thighs with the glaze and continue to cook until the internal temperature of the chicken reaches 175 to 180°F (79 to 82°C), 30 to 40 minutes. Remove the chicken from the smoker and let it rest for 5 minutes before serving.

Smoked Beef Plate Ribs
Makes 4 to 5 servings

At first glance, these giant beef ribs can seem a little intimidating. However, they are easy to make on the EGG. Just give them a dusting of beef rub before they hit the smoke. These are the kind of rich, tender, melt-in-your-mouth ribs that will satisfy that primal urge to gnaw meat from a bone.

SIMPLE BEEF RUB

2 tbsp (38 g) kosher salt

2 tbsp (12 g) freshly ground black pepper

2 tsp (5 g) granulated garlic

2 tsp (5 g) onion powder

2 tsp (5 g) smoked paprika

1 (5- to 6-lb [2.3- to 2.7-kg]) 3-bone beef plate rib

2 tbsp (30 ml) olive oil

1 cup (240 ml) beef stock

Prepare the rub: In a medium-sized bowl, combine all the rub ingredients, then set aside.

Set up the EGG to cook at 300°F (150°C), indirect with a drip pan. Fill your firebox with natural lump charcoal, layering it with three chunks of smoking wood. Hickory or pecan work great here. With the top and bottom vents wide open, light the fire and close the lid. After about 10 minutes, close the bottom draft screen. As the dome temperature approaches your target temperature of 300°F (150°C), about 5 minutes, partially close the bottom vent door and the top of the daisy wheel, leaving both vents 20 percent open. Make minor adjustments as necessary.

Prepare the meat: Trim the fat and silver skin from the meaty side of the ribs. Remove the membrane from the bone side and rub all over with the olive oil. Season the ribs with an even layer of the beef rub to coat all sides.

Once the cooker comes up to temperature, place the ribs, bone side down, on the cooking grid. Close the lid and cook the ribs undisturbed until they reach an internal temperature of 165 to 175°F (73 to 79°C), about 3 hours. Using heavy insulated gloves, place the ribs in a disposable pan fitted with a wire rack. Pour the beef stock around the ribs, being careful not to pour the liquid on top of the ribs. Wrap the pan with aluminum foil and place it on the grill to cook until the ribs reach an internal temperature of 203 to 208°F (95 to 98°C), about 2 hours. Probe the ribs between the bones to check for tenderness; you should feel little resistance as the thermometer slides in and out. Remove the ribs from the cooker and open the foil to vent for 5 minutes. Using heavy insulated gloves, transfer the ribs to a new sheet of foil. Fold up the sides to wrap and place the ribs in a dry cooler to rest for about an hour.

Use a large knife to slice between the bones and arrange on a platter to serve.

Pork Belly Burnt Ends

Makes 16 to 20 servings

I love smoking pork belly burnt ends on the EGG. They require minimal effort to prepare, and the payoff yields irresistible, caramelized cubes of meat—the same kind that is used to make bacon!

Nonstick spray

1 (4- to 5-lb [1.8- to 2.3-kg]) slab uncured pork belly, skin removed

Sweet and Smoky BBQ Rub (page 110)

¼ cup (55 g/½ stick) unsalted butter, cubed

¼ cup (60 g) packed light brown sugar

2 tbsp (30 ml) honey

GLAZE

1 cup (240 ml) Kansas City BBQ Sauce (page 88)

¼ cup (60 ml) apple juice

¼ cup (80 g) apple jelly

Set up the EGG for 275°F (140°C), indirect with a drip pan. Fill your firebox with natural lump charcoal, layering it with two or three chunks of smoking wood. For pork belly, I like to use either apple or cherry wood. With the top and bottom vents wide open, light the fire and close the EGG. After about 10 minutes, close the bottom draft screen. When the temperature nears your 275°F (140°C) target temperature, partially close the bottom vent door and the top of the daisy wheel, leaving both vents 15 percent open. Make minor adjustments as necessary. Lightly spray a baking rack with nonstick spray.

Using a sharp knife, cut the pork belly into 2-inch (5-cm) squares.

Season the pork all over with the BBQ rub and let it sit out for 30 minutes. Place the pork cubes on the prepared baking rack. This will make it easier to move the meat to and from the smoker.

Once the cooker reaches temperature, place the rack with the pork belly on the grate in the smoker and close the lid. Cook until the pork reaches an internal temperature of 165°F (73°C), about 2½ hours.

Transfer the pork belly from the cooker to a disposable aluminum pan and top it with the butter, brown sugar and honey. Wrap the pan tightly with heavy-duty aluminum foil and return it to the smoker. Continue to cook until the pork reaches an internal temperature of 200°F (100°C), about 1 hour.

Remove the pork belly from the smoker and open the foil to vent for 10 minutes.

Prepare the glaze: In a small saucepan, over medium heat, combine the BBQ sauce, apple juice and apple jelly. Cook for 5 to 6 minutes, stirring frequently, until slightly thickened. Place the pork cubes in a large bowl and toss with the sauce mixture to coat. Return the pork to the disposable aluminum pan and place it back on the smoker to cook for 20 to 30 minutes to set the sauce.

Remove the pork belly burnt ends from the smoker and let rest for 10 minutes. Arrange on a platter to serve.

Smoky BBQ Meat Loaf

Makes 4 to 6 servings

This meat loaf is the ultimate home-cooked comfort food. It's easy to prepare and will give you every reason to fire up the EGG on a weeknight.

MEAT LOAF

2 lb (905 g) 80/20 ground beef

1 lb (455 g) ground pork

½ cup (80 g) chopped yellow onion

2 tsp (6 g) minced garlic

2 large eggs, beaten

1 tbsp (15 ml) Worcestershire sauce

1 cup (115 g) unseasoned dried bread crumbs

1½ cups (173 g) shredded Cheddar cheese

1 tsp salt

1 tsp freshly ground black pepper

MEAT LOAF GLAZE

½ cup (120 ml) ketchup

¼ cup (60 g) packed light brown sugar

1 tbsp (15 ml) cider vinegar

2 tsp (5 g) chili powder

Nonstick spray

Sweet and Smoky BBQ Rub (page 110)

Prepare the meat loaf: In a large bowl, mix together the ground beef, ground pork, onion, garlic, eggs, Worcestershire sauce, bread crumbs, cheese, salt and black pepper until just combined, being careful not to overmix the meat.

Prepare two loaf pans by lining each pan with a piece of plastic wrap that is twice the size of the pan, leaving the excess wrap hanging over the sides. Cut the meat loaf mixture in half and gently press each half down into a prepared loaf pan. Cover the pans with the overhanging plastic wrap and refrigerate them for 1 hour.

Prepare the glaze: In a small bowl, combine the ketchup, brown sugar, vinegar and chili powder, stirring to dissolve the sugar. Cover and refrigerate until ready to use.

Set up the EGG for 275°F (140°C), indirect with a drip pan. Fill your firebox with natural lump charcoal, layering it with two or three chunks of smoking wood. For beef, I like to use hickory or pecan wood. With the top and bottom vents wide open, light the fire and close the EGG. After about 10 minutes, close the bottom draft screen. When the temperature nears your 275°F (140°C) target temperature, partially close the bottom vent door and the top of the daisy wheel, leaving both vents 15 percent open. Make minor adjustments as necessary.

Spray a baking rack with nonstick spray and place the rack in a disposable aluminum half pan.

Once the cooker reaches temperature, unmold the meat loaves onto the rack-topped pan. Lightly dust the loaves with BBQ rub and place the pan in the smoker. Close the lid and cook for about 1 hour 45 minutes, or until the loaves reach an internal temperature of 150°F (66°C); start checking your temperature at the 90-minute mark. Brush the meat with the glaze and return the pan to the cooker until the loaves reach an internal temperature of 160°F (71°C), about 15 minutes.

Remove the meat loaves from the smoker and let them rest for 10 minutes before slicing.

Herb-Smoked Turkey Breast
with Apple Cranberry Relish
Makes 6 to 8 servings

This herb-smoked turkey breast is perfect for your Thanksgiving table, yet easy enough to make for dinner any time of year. The apple cranberry relish makes for a delicious, sweet, tart accompaniment or topping for leftover turkey sandwiches.

APPLE CRANBERRY RELISH

1½ tsp (8 ml) canola oil

3 tbsp (30 g) chopped red onion

2 large apples, peeled, cored and diced (about 1½ cups [150 g])

1½ tsp (3 g) minced fresh ginger

1 cup (120 g) dried cranberries

1½ tsp (8 ml) honey

1½ cups (355 ml) fresh orange juice

1 (5- to 7-lb [2.3- to 3.2-kg]) bone-in turkey breast

Poultry Brine (page 87)

½ cup (112 g/1 stick) unsalted butter, at room temperature

2 tsp (3 g) minced garlic

2 tsp (2 g) chopped fresh thyme leaves

2 tsp (3 g) chopped fresh rosemary

1 tsp chopped fresh oregano

2 tsp (10 ml) Dijon mustard

1 tsp kosher salt

½ tsp freshly ground black pepper

Nonstick spray

Prepare the apple cranberry relish: In a medium-sized saucepan, heat the oil over medium heat, add the onion and cook until softened, 3 to 4 minutes. Add the apples and ginger and continue to cook until the apples are tender, 5 to 7 minutes. Add the dried cranberries, honey and orange juice to the pan, stirring to combine. Simmer the cranberry mixture until it is slightly thickened, about 25 minutes. Allow the relish to cool, then cover and refrigerate until ready to serve.

Brine the turkey breast: Place the turkey breast in a large, lidded container and pour the brine over the meat to cover. Refrigerate for 12 to 24 hours. Remove the turkey breast from the brine and discard the brine. Rinse the meat under cool running water and pat dry with paper towels.

In a small bowl, combine the butter, garlic, thyme, rosemary, oregano, mustard, salt and pepper. Using your fingers, rub the turkey breast all over with the herb butter, carefully tucking it under the skin.

Spray a baking rack with nonstick spray and place the rack in a disposable aluminum half pan.

Set up the EGG for 300°F (150°C), indirect without a drip pan. Fill your firebox with natural lump charcoal, layering it with three chunks of apple wood and with the top and bottom vents wide open, light the fire and close the EGG. After about 10 minutes, close the bottom draft screen. When the temperature nears your 300°F (150°C) target temperature, partially close the bottom vent door and the top of the daisy wheel, leaving both vents 20 percent open. Make minor adjustments as necessary.

Once the EGG comes up to temperature, place the turkey breast in the rack-topped pan and place it on the cooking grate. Close the lid and cook the turkey, basting it every 30 to 45 minutes, until it reaches an internal temperature of 165°F (73°C), 2 to 2½ hours, depending on the size of the breast. Transfer the turkey breast to a cutting board and let it rest for 15 minutes, before slicing and serving.

CHERRY CHIPOTLE GLAZED HAM

Makes about 15 servings

What's better than having a smoked ham for the holidays? How about a double-smoked ham with a sweet and spicy BBQ glaze? Sounds good to me. What makes it even better is the fact that by cooking it outside on the EGG, there's still plenty of room inside to finish up sides and desserts.

CHERRY CHIPOTLE BBQ SAUCE

2 cups (475 ml) ketchup

1 cup (320 g) cherry preserves

1 cup (240 ml) unsweetened cherry juice

½ cup (115 g) light brown sugar

3 tbsp (45 ml) cider vinegar

1 chipotle pepper (from canned chipotles in adobo sauce)

1 tbsp (15 ml) adobo sauce (from canned chipotles)

1 tbsp (15 ml) Worcestershire sauce

2 tsp (5 g) granulated garlic

1 tsp onion powder

1 (8- to 9-lb [3.6- to 4-kg]) fully-cooked, sliced spiral ham

Sweet and Smoky BBQ Rub (page 110)

Prepare the BBQ sauce: In a medium-sized saucepan, combine all the sauce ingredients. Bring to a gentle boil over medium heat, stirring to dissolve the preserves. Lower the heat to low and simmer, stirring occasionally, until slightly thickened, 20 to 25 minutes. Remove from the heat, let the sauce cool, transfer to a blender and process until smooth. Pour the sauce into a glass jar and store in the refrigerator until you are ready to use it.

Set up the EGG for 275°F (140°C), indirect with a drip pan. Fill your firebox with natural lump charcoal, layering it with two or three chunks of smoking wood. A fruit wood, such as apple or cherry, works great here. With the top and bottom vents wide open, light the fire and close the EGG. After about 10 minutes, close the bottom draft screen. When the temperature nears your 275°F (140°C) target temperature, partially close the bottom vent door and the top of the daisy wheel, leaving both vents 15 percent open. Make minor adjustments as necessary.

Season the ham all over with the BBQ rub, getting some in between the slices for added flavor, and let it sit at room temperature for 30 minutes.

Reheat the BBQ sauce in a medium-sized saucepan over low heat, stirring occasionally. Keep the sauce warm until you are ready to use it.

Once the cooker reaches temperature, place the ham on the grate in the smoker. Close the lid and cook for 1½ hours, then brush it with the BBQ sauce. Return the ham to the smoker and continue to cook until it reaches an internal temperature of 140°F (60°C), 30 to 40 minutes.

Remove the ham from the smoker and let it rest, loosely covered with foil, for 15 minutes.

To carve the ham: Turn the meat on its bottom so that the meat is facing up. Using a long knife, cut around the bone. Then, cut through the natural breaks in the ham where the fat lies to separate the meat.

Arrange the ham slices on a platter to serve.

BARBECUE BEEF SANDWICHES

Makes 8 to 10 servings

These barbecue beef sandwiches are perfect for your next tailgate or anytime you want to feed a small crowd. Tender chuck roast is bathed in smoke, then braised in beer for a winning combination of flavors.

Olive oil

1 (4-lb [1.8-kg]) beef chuck roast

Kosher salt

Freshly ground black pepper

1 large onion, sliced

1 cup (240 ml) low-sodium beef stock

1 cup (240 ml) beer

¼ cup (60 ml) Kansas City BBQ Sauce (page 88), warmed

TO ASSEMBLE

Toasted sandwich buns

Pickles

Sliced white onions

Set up the EGG to cook at 250°F (120°C), indirect with a drip pan. Fill your firebox with natural lump charcoal, layering it with three or four chunks of hickory or pecan wood. With the top and bottom vents wide open, light the fire and close the lid. After about 10 minutes, close the bottom draft screen. As the dome temperature approaches your target temperature of 250°F (120°C), about 5 minutes, partially close the bottom vent door and the top of the daisy wheel, leaving both vents 10 percent open. Make minor adjustments as necessary.

Apply a thin coat of olive oil to the chuck roast and season it with an even layer of salt and pepper. Let it sit at room temperature for 30 minutes.

Once the cooker reaches temperature, place the chuck roast in the smoker and close the lid. Cook for 3 hours, or until it reaches an internal temperature of 150°F (66°C).

Spread the sliced onion on the bottom of a disposable aluminum half pan and top with the chuck roast, beef stock and beer. Cover the pan with heavy-duty aluminum foil and place the pan on the EGG. Cook until the meat reaches an internal temperature of 200 to 205°F (93 to 95°C), 2 to 3 hours. Remove the pan from the smoker and open the foil to vent for 10 minutes. Strain the accumulated juices of their fat and set aside, and refrigerate the jus for 2 to 3 hours, reserving the pan for later use.

Place the chuck roast in two sheets of aluminum foil and then in a clean towel. Place in an empty, dry cooler bin to rest for at least 1 hour.

Once the roast has rested, transfer the reserved cooking liquid to a medium-sized saucepan over medium heat and bring to a simmer.

Place the roast on a large cutting board. Using two forks, shred the meat, discarding any fat that did not render. Place the meat back in the pan it cooked in and combine with the BBQ sauce and ¼ cup (60 ml) of the reserved braising liquid to moisten the meat.

To assemble: Pile the meat on the bottom of toasted buns, then top with pickles, sliced onions and the top bun to serve.

STATE FAIR TURKEY LEGS

Makes 6 servings

If you have ever been to a state or Renaissance fair, chances are you have seen people walking around, gnawing on these giant smoked turkey legs. They are a lean, smoky barbecue treat. I still remember my first time trying them. We were competing at the Triple Threat BBQ, Beer and Music Festival in Harrington, Delaware, at the state fairgrounds.

POULTRY BRINE

1 gal (3.8 L) warm water (110°F [43°C])

½ cup (150 g) kosher salt

⅔ cup (133 g) sugar

¼ cup (8 g) dried sage

1 bay leaf

1 tbsp (5 g) whole peppercorns

1 tbsp (5 g) whole allspice

6 large turkey legs

Olive oil

POULTRY RUB

1 tbsp (8 g) chili powder

1 tbsp (19 g) kosher salt

1 tbsp (6 g) freshly ground black pepper

1 tbsp (7 g) granulated garlic

1 tbsp (7 g) paprika

2 tsp (5 g) onion powder

2 tsp (2 g) ground thyme

1 tsp rubbed sage

Prepare the brine: In a large, lidded container whisk together the warm water, salt and sugar until the sugar and salt are dissolved. Add the sage, bay leaf, peppercorns and allspice; stir to combine. Refrigerate until ready to use. The brine can be made up to 4 days ahead of time. Strain it before use.

Brine the turkey legs: Place the turkey legs in a large, lidded container and pour the brine over the meat to cover. Refrigerate for 12 to 24 hours. Remove the turkey legs from the brine and discard the brine. Rinse the meat under cool running water and pat dry with paper towels.

Prepare the rub: In a small bowl, combine all the rub ingredients. Leftover rub may be stored in an airtight container for up to 6 months.

Set up the EGG for 300°F (150°C), indirect with a drip pan. Fill your firebox with natural lump charcoal, layering it with three chunks of hickory wood and with the top and bottom vents wide open, light the fire and close the EGG. After about 10 minutes, close the bottom draft screen. When the temperature nears your 300°F (150°C) target temperature, partially close the bottom vent door and the top of the daisy wheel, leaving both vents 20 percent open. Make minor adjustments as necessary.

Brush the turkey legs with a thin layer of olive oil, then apply an even layer of the rub to season the meat. Once the cooker reaches temperature, place the turkey legs directly on the cooking grid. Close the lid and cook until the legs reach an internal temperature of 175 to 180°F (79 to 82°C), 2 to 2½ hours.

Transfer the turkey legs to a platter and tent loosely with foil. Let rest for 5 minutes before serving.

Smoked Scotch Eggs
Makes 8 servings

This is my barbecue version of the Scotch eggs recipe I learned how to make in culinary school. It features a sweet and smoky BBQ rub, as well as a rich BBQ glaze. No bread crumbs or frying necessary.

KANSAS CITY BBQ SAUCE

2 cups (475 ml) ketchup

½ cup (120 g) packed light brown sugar

⅓ cup (80 ml) molasses

¼ cup (60 ml) cider vinegar

2 tbsp (30 ml) prepared yellow mustard

1 tbsp (15 ml) Worcestershire sauce

2 tbsp (16 g) onion powder

2 tsp (5 g) chili powder

1½ tsp (4 g) granulated garlic

1 tsp freshly ground black pepper

¼ tsp cayenne pepper

2 tsp (10 ml) natural hickory liquid smoke

2 lb (905 g) breakfast sausage meat

8 hard-boiled large eggs, peeled

Sweet and Smoky BBQ Rub (page 110)

Prepare the sauce: In a medium-sized saucepan, combine all the sauce ingredients and bring to a gentle boil over medium heat, stirring to dissolve the sugar. Lower the heat to low and simmer, stirring occasionally, until slightly thickened, 5 to 8 minutes. Remove from the heat, let cool, transfer to a jar and store it in the refrigerator until ready to use. Leftover sauce can be stored in the refrigerator for up to a month.

Set up the EGG to cook at 275°F (140°C), indirect with a drip pan. Fill your firebox with natural lump charcoal, layering it with two chunks of smoking wood. For this recipe, I like to use hickory wood, but a fruit wood would work here as well. With the top and bottom vents wide open, light the fire and close the lid. After about 10 minutes, close the bottom draft screen. As the dome temperature approaches your target temperature of 275°F (140°C), about 5 minutes, partially close the bottom vent door and the top of the daisy wheel, leaving both vents 15 percent open. Make minor adjustments as necessary.

Divide the sausage into eight equal portions. Using the palm of your hand, gently press down to flatten the meat. Place an egg into the center of each portion and wrap the meat completely around the egg, using your fingers to seal up the edges. Season the sausage-wrapped eggs with an even dusting of the BBQ rub.

Once the smoker comes up to temperature, place the eggs directly on the grid and close the lid. Cook until the internal temperature of the sausage reaches 160°F (71°C), 60 to 70 minutes.

In a medium-sized saucepan, reheat the BBQ sauce over low heat, stirring occasionally. Brush the eggs with the BBQ sauce, close the lid and continue to cook for about 10 minutes to set the sauce. Transfer the eggs to a platter and allow them to rest for 5 minutes before serving.

SMOKED QUESO BEER DIP

Makes 10 to 12 servings

This queso dip is a fun BBQ appetizer that comes together quickly on the EGG. It's perfect for the big game or anytime that you are craving a cheesy, smoky snack.

1 lb (455 g) cooked, ground sausage (your choice of hot, sweet or breakfast; without casing)

1 lb (455 g) cubed Velveeta

8 oz (225 g) cubed Monterey Jack cheese

½ cup (58 g) shredded sharp Cheddar cheese

1 medium-sized onion, diced

1 medium-sized green bell pepper, seeds and ribs removed, diced

1 jalapeño pepper, seeds and ribs removed, minced

1 (10-oz [280-g]) can diced tomatoes with green chiles (mild or hot; I use Ro-Tel brand)

1 (4-oz [115-g]) can diced green chiles (mild or hot)

1½ tsp (4 g) ground cumin

½ tsp dried oregano

⅛ tsp granulated garlic

⅛ tsp onion powder

1 tbsp (3 g) chopped fresh cilantro

12 oz (355 ml) beer, your favorite

Optional fixings: cilantro, scallions, pickled jalapeños

Tortilla chips, for serving

Set up the EGG for 300°F (150°C), indirect without a drip pan. Fill your firebox with natural lump charcoal, topping it off with two chunks of hickory wood and with the top and bottom vents wide open, light the fire and close the EGG. After about 10 minutes, close the bottom draft screen. When the temperature nears your 300°F (150°C) target temperature, partially close the bottom vent door and the top of the daisy wheel, leaving both vents 20 percent open. Make minor adjustments as necessary.

Once the cooker comes up to temperature, combine all the dip ingredients, except the fixings and tortilla chips, in a large, cast-iron skillet. Place the skillet on the cooking grate, close the lid and cook the queso until the cheese is melted and bubbly, 25 to 30 minutes, stirring occasionally. Remove the queso dip from the grill and top with the fixings (if using). Serve with tortilla chips for dipping.

Slow Fire

ROASTING, INDIRECT GRILLING

One of my favorite ways to cook meats, vegetables and sides is over the slow fire of a kamado-style grill. This method of charcoal roasting on the Big Green Egg adds another layer of flavor, like the subtle notes of smoke provided by a wood-burning oven. The food is cooked indirectly, with temperatures that generally range from 300 to 450°F (150 to 230°C). While the higher cooking temperature helps promote browning and caramelization, the hot air circulates around the food, ensuring that it cooks evenly on all sides. This indirect grilling setup is very much like the EGG setup for smoking; however, no smoking wood is used to flavor the food. This is the perfect way to cook fun and delicious comfort foods on your grill. Are you in the mood for a New Orleans–Style Barbecue Shrimp appetizer (page 105) or Dry-Rubbed Hot Wings with BBQ Ranch Dressing (page 109)? How about Savory Roast Beef with Mushroom Gravy (page 94) or Creamy au Gratin Potatoes (page 121)? In this chapter, I will show you how to make these satisfying dishes and more on your Big Green Egg. You may never want to use your kitchen oven again!

Savory Roast Beef *with* Mushroom Gravy
Makes 8 to 10 servings

This roast beef might sound fancy and complicated to make, but it's actually quite simple. Generously season a good cut of meat, at least choice grade or higher. Place it on the grate, close the lid and let the EGG do all the work. Once the meat is done cooking, allow it to rest, then slice it against the grain to ensure tenderness.

ROAST BEEF RUB

1 tbsp (3 g) dried oregano

1 tbsp (3 g) ground thyme

2 tsp (2 g) dried, crushed rosemary

2 tsp (5 g) granulated garlic

2 tsp (5 g) onion powder

1 tsp dry mustard

2 tsp (13 g) kosher salt

1 tsp freshly ground black pepper

1 (4-lb [1.8-kg]) top round or eye round roast

Olive oil

MUSHROOM GRAVY

2 tbsp (28 g) unsalted butter

1 (8-oz [225-g]) package sliced mushrooms

2 tbsp (15 g) all-purpose flour

¼ cup (60 ml) red wine

2 cups (475 ml) beef stock

Kosher salt

Freshly ground black pepper

Set up the EGG for 375°F (190°C), indirect with a drip pan. Fill your firebox with natural lump charcoal and with the top and bottom vents wide open, light the fire and close the EGG. After about 10 minutes, close the bottom draft screen. When the temperature nears your 375°F (190°C) target temperature, partially close the bottom vent door and the top of the daisy wheel, leaving both vents 35 percent open. Make minor adjustments as necessary.

Prepare the rub: In a small bowl, stir together all the rub ingredients, then set aside.

Trim the roast of any loose or hanging fat. Rub the meat all over with a thin coating of olive oil, and season it generously with the rub.

Once the cooker is up to temperature, place the roast on the grate and close the lid. Roast the beef until it reaches an internal temperature of 125°F (52°C) for medium rare, 75 to 80 minutes.

While the roast is cooking, prepare the gravy: In a medium-sized saucepan, melt the butter over medium heat. Add the mushrooms to the pan and cook, stirring occasionally, until most of the moisture evaporates. Add the flour and cook, stirring often, for 2 to 3 minutes. Slowly stir in the wine and stock. Season the gravy with salt and pepper to taste and bring it to a gentle boil. Lower the heat to low and simmer until it is slightly thickened, stirring occasionally, 8 to 10 minutes. Keep warm until ready to serve.

When the roast is ready, transfer it to a cutting board and tent loosely with foil. Allow the meat to rest for 15 minutes. Using a sharp knife, slice the roast thinly against the grain and arrange the slices on a platter. Serve with the mushroom gravy on the side.

Fontina-Stuffed Meatballs
with Blistered Tomato–Basil Sauce

Makes 4 to 6 servings

These cheese-stuffed meatballs are always a hit at our house. The fact that I can make the whole meal on the Big Green Egg, including the flavorful rustic tomato sauce, is a huge bonus.

1½ lb (680 g) ground meat loaf mix (pork, beef and veal)

¾ cup (86 g) seasoned dry bread crumbs

⅓ cup (33 g) grated Parmesan cheese

2 large eggs

1 tbsp (4 g) chopped fresh parsley

2 cloves garlic, minced

2 tsp (4 g) Italian seasoning

Kosher salt

Freshly ground black pepper

5½ oz (155 g) fontina cheese, cut into ¼" (6-mm) cubes

TOMATO BASIL SAUCE

1 tbsp (15 ml) extra-virgin olive oil

5 cups (750 g) cherry tomatoes

8 to 10 cloves garlic, crushed with the back of a knife

Kosher salt

Freshly ground black pepper

Fresh basil leaves, torn

TO SERVE

Fresh basil leaves

Grated Parmigiano-Reggiano cheese (optional)

In a large bowl, combine the meat loaf mix, bread crumbs, Parmesan cheese, eggs, parsley, garlic and Italian seasoning, then generously season with salt and pepper. Scoop the meat mixture into twelve 2-ounce (55-g) portions. Press one cube of the fontina cheese into each portion and roll into a ball to seal the edges. Place the meatballs on a sheet pan, cover and refrigerate them until you are ready to cook.

Set up the EGG for 375°F (190°C), indirect with a drip pan. Fill your firebox with natural lump charcoal and with the top and bottom vents wide open, light the fire and close the EGG. After about 10 minutes, close the bottom draft screen. When the temperature nears your 375°F (190°C) target temperature, partially close the bottom vent door and the top of the daisy wheel, leaving both vents 35 percent open. Make minor adjustments as necessary.

Place a Dutch oven on the cooking grid to preheat it for 15 minutes.

Prepare the tomato basil sauce: In the Dutch oven, heat the oil until it shimmers, then add the tomatoes, stirring to coat them with the oil. Sear the tomatoes for 3 to 4 minutes, then add the garlic, stirring to combine. Close the lid and cook until the tomatoes are tender and have released most of their juices, about 25 minutes. Using the back of a large spoon, crush half of the tomatoes in the pan and season them with salt and pepper to taste. Add the torn basil leaves and give the sauce a stir to incorporate them. Remove the tomato sauce from the grill and keep it warm until you are ready to serve.

Place the meatballs on the cooking grid and close the lid. Cook until the internal temperature of the meatballs reaches 160°F (71°C), about 30 minutes.

Arrange the meatballs on a platter and top them with the tomato basil sauce, basil leaves and Parmigiano-Reggiano (if using).

PRIME RIB ROAST
with HORSERADISH MUSTARD SAUCE
Makes 6 to 8 servings

I love making prime rib on the EGG. Its delicious golden-brown crust and juicy pink interior make this showstopper the perfect choice for your holiday table or a Sunday dinner, with even better leftover sandwiches.

HORSERADISH MUSTARD SAUCE

1¼ cups (281 g) mayonnaise

¼ cup (44 g) Dijon mustard

2 tbsp (30 g) prepared horseradish

½ cup (115 g) sour cream

Kosher salt

Freshly ground black pepper

1 (7-lb [3.2-kg]) rib-eye roast, bone in (see Note)

Olive oil

Kosher salt

Freshly ground black pepper

Granulated garlic

Note: Ask the butcher to cut the meat off the bones and tie it back on. This will help in the carving process once the roast is cooked.

Prepare the horseradish mustard sauce: In a medium-sized bowl, whisk together the mayonnaise, mustard, horseradish and sour cream. Season the sauce with salt and pepper to taste. Cover and store in the refrigerator until you are ready to serve it.

Rub the roast all over with olive oil and season it generously with the salt, pepper and granulated garlic. Let it sit out at room temperature while you fire up the EGG, for up to an hour.

Set up the EGG for 350°F (180°C), indirect with a drip pan. Fill your firebox with natural lump charcoal and with the top and bottom vents wide open, light the fire and close the EGG. After about 10 minutes, close the bottom draft screen. When the temperature nears your 350°F (180°C) target temperature, partially close the bottom vent door and the top of the daisy wheel, leaving both vents 30 percent open. Make minor adjustments as necessary.

Once the EGG comes up to temperature, place the roast, bone side down, on the grate. Close the lid and cook until the internal temperature of the meat reaches 125°F (52°C) for medium rare, 1½ to 2 hours.

Transfer the roast to a platter and tent it loosely with foil. Allow the meat to rest for 25 to 30 minutes. The internal temperature of the meat will rise 7 to 10°F (4 to 6°C) during this time.

To carve the prime rib: Remove the butcher's twine (see Note) and cut the meat away from the bones. Place the roast, cut side down, on a cutting board and slice the meat against the grain into 1-inch (2.5-cm)-thick slices. Arrange the prime rib slices on a platter and serve them with the horseradish mustard sauce.

Separate the ribs by slicing in between the bones. Serve the ribs along with the meat or reserve them for later.

Pork Tenderloin with Apple-Bourbon BBQ Sauce

Makes 4 servings

With a few simple preparations and a quick cook on the EGG, you will never have to sit through a dinner of dried-out, flavorless pork tenderloin again. Pork and apples may be a traditional pairing, but once you add sweet and smoky bourbon to the mix, all bets are off. The subtle notes of caramel and spice in the glaze push this dish over the top.

APPLE-BOURBON BBQ SAUCE

1 cup (240 ml) ketchup

1 tbsp (11 g) prepared yellow mustard

1 tbsp (15 ml) cider vinegar

1 tbsp (15 g) light brown sugar

2 tbsp (30 ml) pure maple syrup

3 tbsp (45 ml) bourbon

¼ cup (60 ml) apple juice

1 tsp Worcestershire sauce

½ tsp fresh lemon juice

½ tsp ground cinnamon

½ tsp granulated garlic

1 tsp onion powder

½ tsp paprika

¼ tsp red pepper flakes

2 pork tenderloins, about 1½ lb (680 g) each, silver skin removed

Olive oil

Kosher salt

Freshly ground black pepper

Prepare the BBQ sauce: In a small saucepan combine all the sauce ingredients and bring to a gentle boil over medium heat, stirring frequently. Lower the heat to low and simmer until the sauce is slightly thickened, 5 to 8 minutes.

Set up the EGG for 400°F (200°C), indirect with a drip pan. Fill your firebox with natural lump charcoal and with the top and bottom vents wide open, light the fire and close the EGG. After about 10 minutes, close the bottom draft screen. When the temperature nears your 400°F (200°C) target temperature, partially close the bottom vent door and the top of the daisy wheel, leaving both vents 40 percent open. Make minor adjustments as necessary.

Prepare the pork tenderloins: Rub the tenderloins down with a light coating of olive oil and season with salt and black pepper. Once the EGG comes up to temperature, place the pork on the cooking grid and close the lid. Cook for about 14 minutes, then brush the tenderloins with the BBQ sauce and continue to cook until they reach an internal temperature of 145°F (63°C), 5 to 6 minutes. Remove the tenderloins from the grill, tent loosely with foil and allow them to rest for 10 minutes before slicing and serving.

Bacon-Wrapped Jalapeño Chicken Bombs

Makes 8 servings

Who says you can't have your favorite game day snack for dinner any night of the week? These creamy and spicy chicken breasts are loaded with all the flavors you expect from a jalapeño popper, plus bacon and BBQ sauce!

4 thick, boneless and skinless chicken breasts

4 oz (115 g) cream cheese, at room temperature

1 cup (115 g) shredded Cheddar cheese

4 jalapeño peppers, cut in half lengthwise and seeded

16 slices bacon

Sweet and Smoky BBQ Rub (page 110)

1 cup (240 ml) Kansas City BBQ Sauce, warmed (page 88)

Prep the chicken: Using a sharp knife, cut the chicken breasts in half horizontally. Place each half between two pieces of waxed paper, and using a meat mallet, pound the chicken to ¼-inch (6-mm) thickness.

In a small bowl, combine the cream cheese and Cheddar cheese. Fill each jalapeño half with 1 tablespoon (22 g) of the cheese mixture. Place one stuffed jalapeño half, cheese side down, on the short end of a chicken breast and roll it up. Wrap each chicken bundle with 2 slices of bacon, and secure them with toothpicks, if necessary. Season the bundles all over with an even layer of the rub. Refrigerate the bundles until you are ready to cook them.

Set up the EGG for 350°F (180°C), indirect with a drip pan. Fill your firebox with natural lump charcoal and with the top and bottom vents wide open, light the fire and close the EGG. After about 10 minutes, close the bottom draft screen. When the temperature nears your 350°F (180°C) target temperature, partially close the bottom vent door and the top of the daisy wheel, leaving both vents 30 percent open. Make minor adjustments as necessary.

Once the cooker is up to temperature, place the chicken bombs on the cooking grate and close the lid. Cook until the chicken reaches an internal temperature of 165°F (73°C), about 30 minutes, brushing the chicken with the BBQ sauce during the last 5 minutes of cooking to set the glaze. Remove the chicken from the grill and let rest for 10 minutes before serving.

New Orleans–Style Barbecue Shrimp

Makes 6 to 8 servings

In New Orleans, preparing barbecue shrimp is all about the piquant butter sauce that the shrimp are cooked in. Serve this easy and addictive shrimp dish as an appetizer with plenty of crusty bread to soak up the sauce or with rice as a main.

12 oz (355 ml) lager-style beer

3 tbsp (23 g) Creole seasoning

½ cup (120 ml) Worcestershire sauce

⅓ cup (80 ml) fresh lemon juice

1 medium-sized shallot, minced

3 tbsp (12 g) chopped fresh parsley

1 tbsp (10 g) minced garlic

2 tsp (10 ml) hot sauce, such as Crystal brand

Freshly ground black pepper

1 cup (225 g/2 sticks) unsalted butter, cut into 1" (2.5-cm) cubes, chilled

2 lb (905 g) jumbo shrimp (16–20 count), peeled and deveined, tail on

TO SERVE

Thinly sliced scallions

Lemon wedges

Set up the EGG for 350°F (180°C), indirect without a drip pan. Fill your firebox with natural lump charcoal and with the top and bottom vents wide open, light the fire and close the EGG. After about 10 minutes, close the bottom draft screen. When the temperature nears your 350°F (180°C) target temperature, partially close the bottom vent door and the top of the daisy wheel, leaving both vents 30 percent open. Make minor adjustments as necessary.

Place a large, cast-iron skillet or a Dutch oven on the EGG to preheat for about 15 minutes.

When the pan is hot, stir in the beer, Creole seasoning, Worcestershire sauce, lemon juice, shallot, parsley, garlic, hot sauce and pepper to taste. Close the lid and allow the mixture to simmer for 3 to 4 minutes. Using heavy insulated gloves, remove the pan from the heat and whisk in the butter to make a sauce.

Add the shrimp to the pan, stirring to coat them. Place the pan on the cooking grate and close the lid. Cook until the shrimp are pink and firm to the touch with a little give, 8 to 10 minutes.

Remove the shrimp from the grill and garnish with sliced scallions and lemon wedges. Serve immediately.

Note: If you want to kick up the flavor, you can use the traditional method of cooking and serving the shrimp unpeeled, with the head and tail still on. Just make sure you have plenty of napkins; it can get a bit messy.

Chicken Shawarma *with* Yogurt-Tahini Sauce

Makes 4 servings

Since my favorite Middle Eastern restaurant closed, I have been on a quest to recreate those warm, fragrant flavors at home. Traditional shawarma calls for roasting meat on a large vertical spit. You can mimic that effect by roasting marinated dark meat chicken on the EGG, using high heat to get the chicken crisp on the outside, while keeping it moist and juicy on the inside.

MARINADE

1 tbsp (7 g) ground cumin

2 tsp (4 g) ground coriander

1 tsp ground turmeric

2 tsp (5 g) smoked paprika

½ tsp ground cinnamon

½ tsp cayenne pepper

2 tsp (4 g) ground cardamom

2 tsp (12 g) salt

2 tsp (6 g) minced garlic

⅓ cup (80 ml) olive oil

2 tsp (4 g) lemon zest

2 tbsp (30 ml) fresh lemon juice

2 lb (905 g) boneless and skinless chicken thighs

YOGURT-TAHINI SAUCE

1 cup (230 g) Greek yogurt

1 tsp minced garlic

2 tbsp (30 ml) tahini

½ tsp ground cumin

1 tsp dried dill

2 tbsp (30 ml) fresh lemon juice

Kosher salt

Freshly ground black pepper

Optional fixings: romaine lettuce, cucumbers, tomatoes, warmed pitas

Prepare the marinade: In a medium-sized bowl combine the cumin, coriander, turmeric, paprika, cinnamon, cayenne, cardamom, salt, garlic, olive oil, lemon zest and lemon juice. Place the chicken thighs in a large ziplock bag and pour the marinade over it to coat the chicken. Seal the bag and place it in a shallow baking dish in the refrigerator for at least 4 hours and up to overnight.

Prepare the yogurt-tahini sauce: In a small bowl, combine the yogurt, garlic, tahini, cumin, dill, lemon juice and salt and black pepper to taste. Transfer the sauce to a jar and refrigerate until you are ready to use it.

Set up the EGG for 400°F (200°C), indirect without a drip pan. Fill your firebox with natural lump charcoal and with the top and bottom vents wide open, light the fire and close the EGG. After about 10 minutes, close the bottom draft screen. When the temperature nears your 400°F (200°C) target temperature, partially close the bottom vent door and the top of the daisy wheel, leaving both vents 40 percent open. Make minor adjustments as necessary.

Remove the chicken from the marinade and discard the marinade. Place the chicken in a large, cast-iron skillet or baking dish. Once the cooker is up to temperature, place the skillet of chicken on the grate and close the lid. Cook until the chicken reaches an internal temperature of 175 to 180°F (79 to 82°C), 40 to 45 minutes. Transfer to a cutting board and tent loosely with foil. Let the thighs rest for 5 minutes, then cut them into 1-inch (2.5-cm) strips.

To serve: Arrange the sliced chicken on a platter with the yogurt-tahini sauce and your desired fixings.

Dry-Rubbed Hot Wings
with BBQ Ranch Dressing
Makes 6 to 8 servings

These kicked-up hot wings get their robust flavor from the spicy dry rub, no Buffalo sauce required. You will be craving them after the first bite, and not just on game day.

BBQ RANCH DRESSING

⅓ cup (75 g) mayonnaise

¼ cup (60 ml) buttermilk

¼ cup (60 g) sour cream

½ tsp dried dill

½ tsp dried parsley

¼ tsp granulated garlic

½ tsp onion powder

1 cup (240 ml) Kansas City BBQ Sauce (page 88) or store-bought

Kosher salt

Freshly ground black pepper

HOT WING RUB

½ cup (115 g) packed light brown sugar

2 tbsp (14 g) paprika

1 tbsp (8 g) chili powder

1 tbsp (7 g) granulated garlic

2 tsp (5 g) onion powder

2 tsp (6 g) dry mustard

1 tbsp (20 g) kosher salt

1 tbsp (6 g) freshly ground black pepper

¼ tsp dried thyme

2 tsp (4 g) cayenne pepper, or more if you like it hotter

3 lb (1.4 kg) chicken wings, drums and flats

Olive oil

Prepare the ranch dressing: In a medium-sized bowl, combine the mayonnaise, buttermilk, sour cream, dill, parsley, granulated garlic, onion powder, BBQ sauce and salt and black pepper to taste. Whisk until smooth. Transfer the dressing to a jar and store in the refrigerator until ready to use.

Prepare the rub: In a medium-sized bowl, stir together all the rub ingredients, then set aside. Leftover rub may be stored in an airtight container for up to 6 months.

Set up the EGG for 350°F (180°C), indirect with a drip pan. Fill your firebox with natural lump charcoal and with the top and bottom vents wide open, light the fire and close the EGG. After about 10 minutes, close the bottom draft screen. When the temperature nears your 350°F (180°C) target temperature, partially close the bottom vent door and the top of the daisy wheel, leaving both vents 30 percent open. Make minor adjustments as necessary.

In a large bowl, toss the wings with a thin coating of olive oil, then season them with an even layer of the hot wing rub. Once the EGG comes up to temperature, place the wings, skin side down, on the grate. Close the lid and cook for about 25 minutes. Flip the wings so they are skin side up and continue to cook until they reach an internal temperature of 165 to 175°F (73 to 79°C), 25 to 30 minutes.

Transfer the wings to a platter and serve them with a side of BBQ ranch dressing for dipping.

CANDIED BACON

Makes about 6 servings

If you have never tried candied bacon, you are in for a real meat treat. Thick-cut bacon is dredged in brown sugar and seasoned with a sweet and smoky BBQ rub before it goes on the EGG. As the smell of the cooking bacon wafts through the air, you know you will soon be enjoying a sticky sweet bite of BBQ heaven.

SWEET AND SMOKY BBQ RUB

½ cup (115 g) light brown sugar

2 tbsp (12 g) sea salt

1 tbsp (7 g) smoked paprika

1 tbsp (7 g) granulated garlic

1 tbsp (8 g) onion powder

2 tsp (4 g) freshly ground black pepper

2 tsp (6 g) dry mustard

½ tsp ancho chili powder

½ tsp cayenne pepper

Nonstick spray

1 cup (225 g) light brown sugar

1 lb (455 g) thick-cut bacon (see Note)

Prepare the rub: In a small bowl, combine all the rub ingredients. Mix well, then set aside. Any leftover rub may be stored in an airtight container for up to 6 months.

Set up the EGG to cook at 325°F (170°C), indirect with a drip pan. Fill your firebox with natural lump charcoal. With the top and bottom vents wide open, light the fire and close the lid. After about 10 minutes, close the bottom draft screen. As the dome temperature approaches your target temperature of 325°F (170°C), about 5 minutes, partially close the bottom vent door and the top of the daisy wheel, leaving both vents 25 percent open. Make minor adjustments as necessary.

Spray a wire rack with nonstick spray. Place the brown sugar in a 1-gallon (3.8-L) ziplock bag. Toss the bacon slices, one at a time, in the bag to coat and place on the prepared wire rack. Dust each slice with the BBQ rub on both sides.

Place the rack of bacon in the EGG and cook for 15 minutes. Carefully flip each slice of bacon over and close the lid. Cook for another 15 minutes and check the bacon for doneness. You want it to be as well done as you can get it without burning it.

Cook for 5 to 10 minutes more, or to your preferred doneness. Remove the rack from the cooker and immediately transfer the bacon slices to a rack-topped sheet pan to cool. Make sure the bacon slices do not touch while cooling, as they could stick together. Allow the bacon slices to cool for 5 minutes before serving.

Store leftover candied bacon wrapped in parchment paper or foil in the refrigerator for up to 3 days.

Note: While you can achieve great results with regular store-bought bacon, my favorite is Bill-E's Small Batch Bacon from Fairhope, Alabama.

Pig Mac and Cheese

Makes 8 to 10 servings

This rich and creamy bacon mac and cheese has everything you need to amp up the side dish game at your next cookout. It is loaded with porky goodness, from the smoky bacon inside, to the crushed pork rinds on top.

5 tbsp (70 g) unsalted butter, plus more for baking dish

2 cups (225 g) shredded sharp Cheddar cheese, divided

2 cups (225 g) shredded Gouda cheese, divided

1 cup (115 g) shredded Colby Jack cheese, divided

¾ cup (15 g) crushed pork rinds (see Note)

¼ cup (15 g) panko bread crumbs

8 oz (225 g) thick-cut bacon, chopped

6 tbsp (45 g) all-purpose flour

½ tsp kosher salt

¼ tsp freshly ground black pepper

¼ tsp dry mustard

¼ tsp onion powder

4 cups (946 ml) milk

1 lb (455 g) medium-sized macaroni shells, cooked al dente

Note: To crush the pork rinds, place them in a 1-gallon (3.8-L) ziplock bag. Use a rolling pin to break them into small pieces.

Set up the EGG for 375°F (190°C), indirect without a drip pan. Fill your firebox with natural lump charcoal and with the top and bottom vents wide open, light the fire and close the EGG. After about 10 minutes, close the bottom draft screen. When the temperature nears your 375°F (190°C) target temperature, partially close the bottom vent door and the top of the daisy wheel, leaving both vents 35 percent open. Make minor adjustments as necessary.

Butter a 9 x 13–inch (23 x 33–cm) baking dish, then set aside.

In a medium-sized bowl combine ¾ cup (86 g) of the Cheddar, ¾ cup (86 g) of the Gouda, ¼ cup (29 g) of the Colby Jack, the pork rinds and panko bread crumbs. Set aside.

In a large, heavy-bottomed pot, cook the bacon over medium heat until browned and crisp, about 5 to 6 minutes. Transfer to a paper towel–lined plate to drain any excess grease. Divide the bacon into two portions.

Remove all but 1 tablespoon (15 g) of bacon grease from the pot and add the 5 tablespoons (70 g) of butter. Allow it to melt. Whisk in the flour and cook for 2 to 3 minutes. Add the salt, pepper, dry mustard and onion powder, stirring to combine. Slowly pour in the milk, whisking constantly while cooking until the mixture thickens, about 5 minutes.

Stir in the remaining cheeses and allow them to melt, adding one portion of the cooked bacon and the cooked pasta. Pour the macaroni and cheese mixture into the prepared baking dish and top with the reserved cheese mixture and the remaining portion of cooked bacon.

Once the EGG comes up to temperature, place the dish on the grate, close the lid and cook for 25 to 30 minutes, or until golden brown and bubbly.

Remove the dish from the cooker and let it rest for 5 to 10 minutes before serving.

Hasselback Sweet Potatoes with Crushed Pecan Butter

Makes 6 servings

Looking for a new sweet potato recipe? Look no further. These sweet and savory, accordion-style potatoes are an easy and elegant-looking side dish that is only made better by cooking it over a slow fire in your Big Green Egg.

6 medium-sized sweet potatoes

1 cup (225 g/2 sticks) unsalted butter, melted

Kosher salt

½ cup (115 g) packed light brown sugar

½ cup (55 g) finely chopped pecans

¼ cup (60 g) Sweet and Smoky BBQ Rub (page 110)

Set up the EGG for 400°F (200°C), indirect without a drip pan. Fill your firebox with natural lump charcoal and with the top and bottom vents wide open, light the fire and close the EGG. After about 10 minutes, close the bottom draft screen. When the temperature nears your 400°F (200°C) target temperature, partially close the bottom vent door and the top of the daisy wheel, leaving both vents 40 percent open. Make minor adjustments as necessary.

Rinse and scrub the sweet potatoes under cool running water to remove any dirt or debris. Pat them dry with paper towels. Slice each potato on one side to give it a flat edge. This will give it a base and stop it from rolling over in the pan.

Slice each potato into thin slices, leaving ¼ inch (6 mm) at the bottom unsliced. To get uniform cuts, place each sweet potato between the handles of two wooden spoons or two chopsticks as you slice. This will prevent you from cutting all the way through the potato.

Place the sweet potatoes in a large baking dish. Brush them generously with the melted butter, reserving some for later, and season with salt to taste.

Once the EGG comes up to temperature, place the sweet potatoes on the cooking grate and close the lid. Cook the potatoes until the slices begin to fan out a bit, about 45 minutes.

While the potatoes are cooking, prepare the topping: In a small bowl, combine the brown sugar, pecans and BBQ rub.

Brush the sweet potatoes with more of the melted butter and sprinkle them with an even coating of the spiced nut mixture, taking care to get in between the slices. Close the lid and continue cooking until the potatoes are tender and golden brown, 20 to 30 minutes.

Southern Corn Bread Dressing

Makes about 12 servings

This southern corn bread dressing is delicious with turkey, but it isn't just for Thanksgiving. It's also the perfect accompaniment to chicken or ham, when you want a hearty Sunday supper.

Nonstick spray

½ cup (112 g/1 stick) unsalted butter

1 medium-sized onion, diced

4 celery ribs, chopped

1 tbsp (10 g) minced garlic

6 cups (510 g) cubed Skillet Corn Bread (page 139), or an 8"(20-cm) square pan of store-bought, cubed

6 cups (300 g) day-old baguette bread, cubed

2 to 3 cups (475 to 710 ml) chicken stock

3 tbsp (12 g) finely chopped fresh parsley

2 tsp (5 g) poultry seasoning

1 tsp dried thyme

Kosher salt

Freshly ground black pepper

2 large eggs, beaten

Spray a 9 x 13–inch (23 x 33–cm) baking dish with nonstick spray.

Set up the EGG for 375°F (190°C), indirect without a drip pan. Fill your firebox with natural lump charcoal and with the top and bottom vents wide open, light the fire and close the EGG. After about 10 minutes, close the bottom draft screen. When the temperature nears your 375°F (190°C) target temperature, partially close the bottom vent door and the top of the daisy wheel, leaving both vents 35 percent open. Make minor adjustments as necessary.

In a medium-sized sauté pan, melt the butter over medium heat. Add the onion and celery and cook until they begin to soften, about 5 minutes. Add the garlic and cook until fragrant, about 1 minute. Remove the pan from the heat and set aside to cool, about 10 minutes.

In a large bowl, combine the cubed breads and the onion mixture. Stir in 2 cups (475 ml) of the chicken stock, then add the parsley, poultry seasoning, thyme and salt and pepper to taste. Adjust the consistency of the dressing by adding more chicken stock, ¼ cup (60 ml) at a time, if the mixture seems a bit dry. Stir in the beaten eggs until incorporated.

Transfer the corn bread mixture to the prepared baking dish and cover it with foil. Once the EGG is up to temperature, place the baking dish on the grate and close the lid. Cook the casserole for about 30 minutes. Remove the foil and continue to cook until the casserole reaches an internal temperature of 160°F (71°C), 20 to 25 minutes. Remove the dressing from the grill and serve immediately.

Roasted Eggplant and Feta Dip

Makes 8 servings

This Mediterranean-inspired eggplant dip is perfect for entertaining, but it's so good that you may not want to share it! If that's the case, try adding it to your snacks, wraps and sandwiches throughout the week.

1 large eggplant, 2½ to 3 lb (1.1 to 1.4 kg), cut in half lengthwise

1 red or yellow bell pepper, seeded and quartered

1 small onion, peeled and quartered

2 cloves garlic, peeled

1 medium-sized tomato, peeled and seeded (see Note)

Olive oil

Kosher salt

Freshly ground black pepper

¾ cup (113 g) crumbled feta cheese

1 tbsp (15 ml) fresh lemon juice

TO SERVE

Chopped fresh herbs, such as thyme or oregano

Toasted pita chips or grilled bread

Washed and cut fresh vegetables

Set up the EGG for 375°F (190°C), indirect without a drip pan. Fill your firebox with natural lump charcoal and with the top and bottom vents wide open, light the fire and close the EGG. After about 10 minutes, close the bottom draft screen. When the temperature nears your 375°F (190°C) target temperature, partially close the bottom vent door and the top of the daisy wheel, leaving both vents 35 percent open. Make minor adjustments as necessary.

Heat a 6-quart (5.7-L) Dutch oven on the grill for about 20 minutes.

In a large bowl, combine the eggplant, bell pepper, onion, garlic and tomato. Drizzle with olive oil and season with salt and black pepper to taste.

Once the cooker is up to temperature, place just the eggplant halves, skin side down, in the Dutch oven and close the lid. Cook for about 15 minutes, then add the rest of the vegetables to the Dutch oven. Continue to cook until all the vegetables are tender, about 45 minutes.

Transfer the vegetables to a sheet pan and allow them to cool, about 15 minutes. When cool enough to handle, scoop the meat of the eggplant out of its skin and into the bowl of a food processor or blender. Remove and discard the skin from the bell pepper and add the bell pepper, onion, garlic and tomato to the processor. Pulse the mixture a few times to combine, then add the feta cheese, lemon juice and 1 tablespoon (15 ml) of olive oil. Pulse a few times more until the mixture is to your desired consistency.

Top the dip with fresh herbs and serve it with toasted pita chips or grilled bread, and cut fresh vegetables for dipping.

Note: To peel and seed the tomato, cut an X in the bottom, and using a slotted spoon, dip it into boiling water for 15 seconds. Rinse the tomato under cold running water to cool it. Use a paring knife to gently pull away the skin where it has split. Cut the tomato in half and use a spoon to scoop out the seeds.

Creamy au Gratin Potatoes

Makes 8 to 10 servings

If you love potatoes as I do, then you are going to love this French-inspired casserole. It's rich, creamy and comforting. Thinly sliced potatoes are layered with cheese and cream before they are cooked until tender by the radiant heat inside the Big Green EGG. This cheesy gratin will quickly become a dinnertime staple the whole family will enjoy.

2 tbsp (28 g) unsalted butter, plus more for skillet

1½ cups (355 ml) heavy cream

2 cloves garlic, minced

2½ lb (1.1 kg) russet potatoes, peeled and cut crosswise into ¼" (6-mm) slices

Kosher salt

Freshly ground black pepper

2½ cups (283 g) shredded Cheddar cheese, divided

3 tbsp (7 g) thinly sliced scallion

Butter a 12-inch (30-cm) cast-iron skillet, then set aside.

Set up the EGG for 350°F (180°C), indirect without a drip pan. Fill your firebox with natural lump charcoal and with the top and bottom vents wide open, light the fire and close the EGG. After about 10 minutes, close the bottom draft screen. When the temperature nears your 350°F (180°C) target temperature, partially close the bottom vent door and the top of the daisy wheel, leaving both vents 30 percent open. Make minor adjustments as necessary.

In a small saucepan, heat the butter, cream and garlic over medium heat, stirring occasionally, until the butter is melted and the cream is warmed through.

Lay one-third of the potatoes in the bottom of the skillet so they are slightly overlapping. Season the potatoes with salt and pepper. Then pour one-third of the cream mixture over the potatoes, and sprinkle them with one-third of the shredded cheese and one-third of the scallion. Repeat the process for the second and third layers, ending with the final portion of scallion but reserving the last portion of cheese for the next step.

Once the EGG is up to temperature, cover the pan with foil and place it on the cooking grate. Close the lid and cook until the potatoes are tender, about 75 minutes. Remove the foil from the pan and top the potatoes with the remaining cheese. Close the lid and continue to cook until the casserole is golden brown and bubbly, 10 to 15 minutes. Remove the potatoes from the grill and allow them to cool for 5 minutes before serving.

Green Bean Casserole

Makes 6 to 8 servings

Green bean casserole wasn't a staple in our household when I was growing up, but now I can't imagine a Thanksgiving meal without it. Fresh flavors and crisp, tender vegetables update this classic and really make this recipe stand out. Of course, adding a layer of smoky bacon to the crunchy onion topping doesn't hurt, either.

2 lb (455 g) fresh green beans, trimmed

3 tbsp (42 g) unsalted butter

1 small onion, thinly sliced

2 tbsp (15 g) all-purpose flour

Kosher salt

Freshly ground black pepper

½ cup (240 ml) milk

1 cup (225 g) sour cream

8 oz (225 g) cremini mushrooms, quartered

1 cup (115 g) shredded Cheddar cheese

1 (2.8-oz [79-g]) can French fried onions

4 slices bacon, cooked and crumbled

Set up the EGG for 350°F (180°C), indirect without a drip pan. Fill your firebox with natural lump charcoal and with the top and bottom vents wide open, light the fire and close the EGG. After about 10 minutes, close the bottom draft screen. When the temperature nears your 350°F (180°C) target temperature, partially close the bottom vent door and the top of the daisy wheel, leaving both vents 30 percent open. Make minor adjustments as necessary.

Prepare an ice-water bath: In a large bowl, combine 4 cups (560 g) of ice and 4 cups (946 ml) of cold water. Set this aside.

In a large-sized pot, bring 2 quarts (1.9 L) of water to a boil over high heat. Add the green beans to the pot and cook until they are just tender, crisp and bright green, 3 to 4 minutes. Drain the beans and immediately soak them in the ice bath to stop the cooking process. When the green beans are cool, drain them and set aside.

Melt the butter in a large, cast-iron skillet over medium heat. Add the onion and cook, stirring, until tender. Whisk in the flour and season the mixture with salt and pepper to taste. Gradually whisk in the milk, stirring constantly so that no lumps form. Stir in the sour cream and continue to cook over medium heat until the sauce slightly thickens, 2 to 3 minutes. Mix in the green beans and mushrooms, stirring to coat them.

Remove the pan from the heat and stir in half of the cheese and fried onions. Top with the remaining cheese and fried onions, and the cooked bacon.

Place the casserole on the cooking grate and close the lid. Cook until the cheese is melted and the sauce is bubbling around the edges, about 25 minutes.

Maple-Mustard Glazed Carrots

Makes 6 servings

These sweet and tangy carrots will complement just about any meal. You will love the deep concentrated flavors and golden caramelized edges brought on by roasting them over high heat in the EGG.

2 bunches carrots (about 2 lb [905 g]), well scrubbed or peeled, tops trimmed

Olive oil

Kosher salt

Freshly ground black pepper

¼ cup (55 g/½ stick) unsalted butter, melted

1 tbsp (3 g) finely chopped fresh thyme leaves

¼ cup (60 ml) pure maple syrup

1 tbsp (15 ml) Dijon mustard

1 tbsp (15 ml) whole-grain mustard

¼ tsp freshly grated nutmeg

Set up the EGG for 400°F (200°C), indirect without a drip pan. Fill your firebox with natural lump charcoal and with the top and bottom vents wide open, light the fire and close the EGG. After about 10 minutes, close the bottom draft screen. When the temperature nears your 400°F (200°C) target temperature, partially close the bottom vent door and the top of the daisy wheel, leaving both vents 40 percent open. Make minor adjustments as necessary.

Place a large, cast-iron skillet on the cooking grid to preheat for 15 to 20 minutes.

In a large bowl, toss the carrots with olive oil and season them with salt and pepper to taste.

Once the skillet is hot, place the carrots in the pan, close the lid and cook for about 30 minutes, stirring occasionally.

Prepare the glaze: In a small bowl, combine the butter, thyme, maple syrup, mustards and nutmeg, stirring until the mixture has a smooth consistency. Pour the glaze over the carrots, stirring to evenly coat them. Close the lid and continue to cook, stirring occasionally, until the carrots are tender and beginning to caramelize around the edges, 10 to 15 minutes.

Arrange the carrots on a platter to serve.

Baking Savory
ON THE BIG GREEN EGG

When you think about cooking on your Big Green Egg, thoughts of tender, fatty brisket, succulent pork or perfectly grilled steaks likely dominate. However, your kamado-style grill has capabilities that extend much further than the usual grilling and smoking. With the addition of a convEGGtor and a pizza and baking stone, your ceramic cooker becomes a classic brick oven that can produce trattoria-style pizza as well as the finest savory baked goods.

The setup for baking on the EGG is indirect and uses no smoking wood. Cooking temperatures and times are similar to those of your kitchen oven. You can use many of the same racks, pans and cast-iron cookware with great results.

In this chapter, I will show you that baking isn't just for desserts. You will create delicious, flaky Barbecue Beef and Cheese Empanadas with Chipotle Aioli (page 128), learn the secrets to making a thin and crispy Pizza Margherita (page 131), prepare irresistible Skillet Corn Bread with Hot Honey Butter (page 139) and more. These recipes will make you eager to fire up your cooker and put your new savory baking skills to good use.

Barbecue Beef and Cheese Empanadas
with Chipotle Aioli

Makes 8 to 10 servings

These savory Latin-inspired hand pies are the perfect vessel for your leftover 'cue. Serve them as an appetizer or game-day snack. Empanadas can be made the day before you intend to cook; just keep them covered in the refrigerator until you are ready to fire up the EGG.

CHIPOTLE AIOLI

½ cup (155 g) mayonnaise

1 tbsp (15 ml) water

2 tsp (10 ml) fresh lime juice

½ tsp chili powder

1 tsp smoked paprika

2 tsp (10 ml) adobo sauce (from canned chipotle peppers)

Salt

Freshly ground black pepper

1 tbsp (30 ml) olive oil

1 small onion, diced

1 small red bell pepper, seeds and ribs removed, diced

1 lb (455 g) shredded Barbecue Beef (page 84)

1 tsp minced garlic

¼ cup (60 ml) Kansas City BBQ Sauce (page 88)

All-purpose flour, for dusting

2 prepared piecrusts

1 cup (115 g) shredded Cheddar cheese

1 large egg, beaten

Line a sheet pan with parchment paper, then set aside.

Set up the EGG for 375°F (190°C), indirect without a drip pan. Fill your firebox with natural lump charcoal and with the top and bottom vents wide open, light the fire and close the EGG. After about 10 minutes, close the bottom draft screen. When the temperature nears your 375°F (190°C) target temperature, partially close the bottom vent door and the top of the daisy wheel, leaving both vents 35 percent open. Make minor adjustments as necessary.

Prepare the chipotle aioli: In a small bowl, whisk to combine all the sauce ingredients until smooth, seasoning with salt and black pepper to taste. Cover and refrigerate until ready to serve.

In a medium-sized skillet, heat the olive oil over medium heat. Add the onion and bell pepper and cook, stirring occasionally, until they begin to soften, about 5 minutes. Add the shredded beef, garlic and BBQ sauce and continue to cook until the mixture is just warmed through. Remove from the heat and let it cool for a few minutes.

On a lightly floured surface, roll out the piecrusts. Using a large biscuit cutter or small plate, cut 4- to 5-inch (10- to 12.5-cm) circles in the piecrusts. Cut them as close as possible to maximize how many you can get. Leftover dough can be rerolled and cut into more circles.

Spoon 2 tablespoons (about 43 g) of filling in the center of each dough circle, and top with 1 tablespoon (8 g) of shredded cheese. Brush the edges of the circle with water, then fold the dough over to form a semicircle. Press and seal the ends by crimping them with a fork. Place the empanadas on the prepared sheet pan and refrigerate for 30 minutes.

Once the cooker comes up to temperature, brush the empanadas with the beaten egg. Place the empanadas in the EGG and close the lid. Bake until golden brown and crisp, 25 to 30 minutes.

PIZZA MARGHERITA

Makes 6 servings

If you have ever dreamed about re-creating the thinly crusted, Neapolitan-style pizza from your favorite pizza joint, here's your chance. The heavy-duty ceramic interior of the EGG and the heat of the wood coals combine to mimic the workings of a wood-fired oven. Now, the best pizza in town will be made right in your backyard!

All-purpose flour, for dusting

1 lb (455 g) fresh pizza dough

8 oz (225 g) fresh mozzarella cheese

½ cup (120 ml) prepared pizza sauce

Grated Parmigiano-Reggiano cheese, for dusting

Extra-virgin olive oil, for drizzling

Fresh basil leaves, torn

Set up the EGG for 600°F (315°C), indirect without a drip pan. Fill your firebox with natural lump charcoal and with the top and bottom vents wide open, light the fire and close the EGG. After about 10 minutes, close the bottom draft screen. When the temperature nears your 600°F (315°C) target temperature, partially close the bottom vent door and the top of the daisy wheel, leaving both vents 80 percent open. Make minor adjustments as necessary.

For the pizza setup, you want to create an air gap between the convEGGtor and the pizza stone. This will help improve air circulation as well as prevent the stone from becoming too hot. As the temperature in the EGG nears 300°F (150°C), as measured at the dome, add the convEGGtor, legs up, then the cooking grate and then the pizza stone. This will allow the pizza stone time to gradually come up to temperature with the grill.

Sprinkle flour onto a hard, flat work surface and work the dough into a 14- to 16-inch (35- to 40-cm)-diameter disk.

Cut the mozzarella into ½-inch (1.3-cm) slices and dab them with a paper towel to absorb any excess moisture.

Sprinkle a light dusting of flour onto a pizza peel and transfer the dough to the peel.

Top the pizza with the pizza sauce, mozzarella and a dusting of Parmigiano-Reggiano cheese.

Use the peel to slide the pizza directly onto the stone. Close the lid and cook until the dough is crispy and the cheese is melted, 5 to 6 minutes. The timing will depend on how well done you prefer your pizza.

Transfer the pizza to a cutting board. Top with a light drizzle of extra-virgin olive oil and torn basil leaves. Cut into slices and serve immediately.

GARLIC KNOTS
Makes about 24 servings

My family goes crazy for these garlic knots, and I think you will, too! They are soft, slightly chewy and drenched in an addictive garlic butter. Serve them as an appetizer or game day treat with a bowl of marinara for dipping.

Nonstick spray

All-purpose flour, for dusting

1 lb (455 g) fresh pizza dough, at room temperature for 1 hour

½ cup (112 g/1 stick) salted butter

1 tbsp (10 g) minced garlic

¾ tsp dried parsley

½ tsp salt

¼ tsp freshly ground black pepper

Grated Pecorino Romano cheese, for topping

Marinara sauce, for serving

Spray a sheet pan with nonstick spray, then set aside.

Set up the EGG for 500°F (250°C), indirect without a drip pan. Fill your firebox with natural lump charcoal and with the top and bottom vents wide open, light the fire and close the EGG. After about 10 minutes, close the bottom draft screen. When the temperature nears your 500°F (250°C) target temperature, partially close the bottom vent door and the top of the daisy wheel, leaving both vents 65 percent open. Make minor adjustments as necessary.

As the temperature in the EGG nears 300°F (150°C), as measured at the dome, add the convEGGtor, legs up, then the cooking grate and then the pizza stone. This will allow the pizza stone time to gradually come up to temperature with the grill.

Sprinkle flour onto a hard, flat work surface and roll the dough into a 6 x 12–inch (15 x 30–cm) rectangle. Using a sharp knife or pizza cutter, cut the dough into twelve 6-inch (15-cm)-long strips. Stretch and roll each strip until it is 12 inches (30 cm) long. Cut the strips crosswise, making 24 pieces. Tie each strip into a loose knot and place on the prepared pan, spacing them about 2 inches (5 cm) apart. Allow the dough knots to rise in a warm place until they puff up to almost doubled in size, about 20 minutes.

In a small saucepan melt the butter over medium-low heat. Add the garlic and cook, stirring frequently, for 1 to 2 minutes. Remove the pan from the heat, stir in the parsley and season with salt and pepper.

Once the cooker comes up to temperature, brush the knots with half of the butter mixture. Place the pan on the baking stone. Close the lid and cook until the knots are crisped and golden brown, about 15 minutes.

Remove the knots from the grill and brush with the remaining garlic butter. Dust with the Pecorino Romano cheese and arrange them on a platter with a side of marinara sauce for dipping.

Sausage Rolls *with* IPA Mustard BBQ Sauce

Makes 16 servings

If you enjoyed eating pigs in a blanket as a kid, then these "grown-up" sausage rolls will stir up a bit of nostalgia. The puff pastry bakes up crisp and flaky around the savory sausages when cooking them on the EGG. Use your favorite beer to make the BBQ sauce and use the leftover to wash it all down.

IPA MUSTARD BBQ SAUCE

½ cup (112 g/1 stick) unsalted butter

½ cup (80 g) diced sweet onion

2 cloves garlic, minced

2 cups (352 g) whole-grain mustard

½ cup (120 ml) IPA beer

2 tsp (10 ml) Worcestershire sauce

2 tbsp (30 g) light brown sugar

¼ tsp cayenne pepper

Pinch of salt

1 sheet puff pastry, thawed

All-purpose flour, for dusting

1 large egg, beaten

8 smoked sausages, hot links, or bratwurst, cut in half crosswise

Poppy seeds, for topping

Dried onion flakes, for topping

Line a sheet pan with parchment paper, then set aside.

Set up the EGG for 400°F (200°C), indirect without a drip pan. Fill your firebox with natural lump charcoal and with the top and bottom vents wide open, light the fire and close the EGG. After about 10 minutes, close the bottom draft screen. When the temperature nears your 400°F (200°C) target temperature, partially close the bottom vent door and the top of the daisy wheel, leaving both vents 40 percent open. Make minor adjustments as necessary.

Prepare the BBQ sauce: In a small saucepan over medium heat, melt the butter. Add the onion and cook, stirring occasionally, for 5 minutes, or until tender. Add the garlic and cook for 20 seconds. Stir in the mustard, beer, Worcestershire sauce, brown sugar, cayenne and salt. Simmer until slightly thickened, 15 to 20 minutes. Remove from the heat and allow to cool. Once cooled, refrigerate until ready to serve.

Roll out the pastry on a floured surface into a 12 x 19–inch (30 x 48–cm) rectangle. Cut the rectangle in half lengthwise, then cut both smaller rectangles into 8 equal portions, totaling 16 pieces of dough.

Brush one end of the dough with the beaten egg. Lay half of a sausage on the opposite end and roll the sausage up in the pastry, pressing lightly to seal the ends. Place the rolls in the refrigerator for 20 to 30 minutes to firm up the dough.

Once the cooker is up to temperature, transfer the sausage rolls to the prepared sheet pan and prick the tops with a fork. Brush the rolls with beaten egg and sprinkle them with poppy seeds and dried onion flakes. Place the pan on the grill and close the lid. Bake until the sausage reaches an internal temperature of 160°F (71°C) and the pastry is golden brown.

Remove the sausage rolls from the grill and arrange them on a platter with the sauce separate, to serve.

Bacon, Cheddar and Chive Quiche

Makes 6 servings

When I am craving breakfast for dinner, this savory egg pie is my go-to meal. I love that it is packed with protein, and it has the perfect ratio of creamy custard to flaky crust. Pair it with a salad or breakfast potatoes to complete the meal.

1 store-bought frozen pie shell, thawed

5 large eggs

2 cups (475 ml) heavy cream

Kosher salt

Freshly ground black pepper

1 cup (115 g) shredded Cheddar cheese

6 slices bacon, cooked and crumbled

1 tbsp (3 g) minced fresh chives

Set up the EGG for 375°F (190°C) indirect with a drip pan. Fill your firebox with natural lump charcoal and with the top and bottom vents wide open, light the fire and close the EGG. After about 10 minutes, close the bottom draft screen. When the temperature nears your 375°F (190°C) target temperature, partially close the bottom vent door and the top of the daisy wheel, leaving both vents 35 percent open. Make minor adjustments as necessary.

Using a fork, poke the pie shell all over to vent it, then place it on a small sheet pan.

Once the grill is up to temperature, place the sheet pan on the grate and close the lid. Parbake the crust for about 5 minutes. Remove the crust from the grill and let it cool on its pan while you prepare the filling.

In a medium-sized bowl, whisk the eggs with the cream and season with salt and pepper. Layer the cheese, bacon and chives in the pie shell. Pour the egg filling over the cheese and bacon mixture, up to the top of the crust. Carefully place the quiche on the grate and close the lid. Bake until a toothpick pressed into the center of the quiche comes out clean, 35 to 40 minutes. The top of the quiche should be browned and puffed up.

Remove the quiche from the grill and allow it to rest for 5 to 6 minutes. Slice into six pieces and serve warm.

Skillet Corn Bread *with* Hot Honey Butter

Makes 8 servings

This classic buttermilk corn bread is moist, tender and easy to make. The secret to achieving its crisp, golden-brown crust is to pour the batter into a hot buttered skillet before it goes on the EGG to bake. Serve it with hot honey butter for the ultimate sweet heat bite.

HOT HONEY BUTTER

½ cup (112 g/1 stick) unsalted butter, at room temperature

3 tbsp (45 ml) honey

1 tbsp (15 ml) hot sauce, such as Crystal brand

Kosher salt

1½ cups (210 g) cornmeal

1 cup (125 g) all-purpose flour

⅓ cup (67 g) sugar

4 tsp (10 g) baking powder

1 tsp salt

2 cups (475 ml) reduced-fat buttermilk

1 large egg

6 tbsp (84 g/¾ stick) unsalted butter, melted, divided

Prepare the hot honey butter: In a medium-sized bowl, whip the butter, using a handheld mixer, until it is light and fluffy, about 2 minutes. Scrape down the sides of the bowl with a silicone spatula. With the mixer running on medium speed, slowly pour in the honey and hot sauce to combine. Season with salt to taste. Using a spoon or silicone spatula, place the butter mixture on a piece of plastic wrap and roll it into the shape of a log. Twist the ends to seal, then refrigerate for 1 hour or until ready to use.

Set up the EGG for 400°F (200°C), indirect without a drip pan. Fill your firebox with natural lump charcoal and with the top and bottom vents wide open, light the fire and close the EGG. After about 10 minutes, close the bottom draft screen. When the temperature nears your 400°F (200°C) target temperature, partially close the bottom vent door and the top of the daisy wheel, leaving both vents 40 percent open. Make minor adjustments as necessary.

In a large bowl, combine the cornmeal, flour, sugar, baking powder and salt. In a medium-sized bowl, whisk together the buttermilk, egg and 3 tablespoons (42 g) of the butter. Pour the wet mixture over the dry mixture and stir to combine.

Heat a 10-inch (25-cm) cast-iron skillet over low heat for 1 to 2 minutes. Add the remaining 3 tablespoons (42 g) of butter to the skillet and remove the pan from the heat. Swirl the butter in the pan to coat all sides.

Once the EGG comes up to temperature, pour the batter into the warm skillet and place it on the cooking grate. Close the lid and bake until a toothpick inserted into the center comes out clean and the top of the corn bread is golden, about 25 minutes.

Remove the corn bread from the grill and allow it to cool for 5 to 10 minutes before slicing. Serve warm with the hot honey butter.

Baking Sweet
ON THE BIG GREEN EGG

Have you ever heard the phrase "as easy as pie"? While most people know it means that something is simple to do, few realize that the saying originally referred to the eating of a pie, which was considered a pleasurable and easy experience, rather than the making of it. After all, making a pie does take some work.

Baking sweet on the Big Green Egg is a lot like baking savory on it. The food is cooked indirectly and uses no smoking wood. Cooking temperatures and times are similar to those of your kitchen oven. You can use many of the same racks, pans and cast-iron cookware with great results.

It is important to start out with a clean cooker when you are planning to bake sweet items on the EGG. Replace any charcoal that has fat or meat drippings from your last cook; otherwise, your sweet treats will be permeated with the flavor of smoky meat renderings. If your cooker is particularly dirty, it may be a good time for a high-heat burn-off. Typically, I do this the day before I plan on baking.

Long before I entered the barbecue world, I was a baker at Cravings Fine Desserts in Allenhurst, New Jersey. During my time there, I learned the finer points of baking in a professional kitchen. The dishes that I am going to share with you in this chapter were inspired by my experience there. Does the thought of learning how to make a Giant Cinnamon Roll with Bourbon Cream Cheese Frosting (page 153) excite you? How about a sweet, tart Key Lime Pie with Graham Cracker Crust (page 145) or Salted Chocolate Chunk Cookies (page 146)? If you answered yes to any of these questions, grab an apron and fire up your cooker. You don't have to be a professional to bake sweet on the Big Green Egg. I will show you that it is "as easy as pie."

Chocolate Bread Pudding *with* Buttered Rum Sauce

Makes about 8 servings

If you want to impress your guests or need a serious chocolate fix, get this rich and decadent bread pudding on your EGG ASAP! Serve it with the buttery, rum-spiked sauce while it is still warm from the grill, for a cozy and comforting treat.

Nonstick spray

BUTTERED RUM SAUCE

½ cup (112 g/1 stick) unsalted butter

1 cup (225 g) packed light brown sugar

⅓ cup (120 ml) heavy cream

3 tbsp (45 ml) dark rum

½ tsp pure vanilla extract

BREAD PUDDING

2 cups (475 ml) heavy cream

1 cup (240 ml) milk

4 large eggs

¾ cup (150 g) granulated sugar

1½ cups (263 g) semisweet chocolate chips

½ cup (55 g) Dutch-processed cocoa powder

½ tsp salt

2 tsp (10 ml) vanilla extract

1 (1-lb [455-g]) day-old baguette loaf, cut into ½" (1.3-cm) cubes

Spray a 9 x 13–inch (23 x 33–cm) baking pan with nonstick spray, then set aside.

Prepare the rum sauce: In a small saucepan, melt the butter over medium heat. Add the brown sugar, stirring to dissolve it. Pour in the cream, rum and vanilla, stirring to combine. Lower the heat to low and simmer, stirring frequently, until slightly thickened, about 5 minutes. Keep the sauce warm until you are ready to serve it.

Prepare the pudding: In a large saucepan over low heat, whisk together the heavy cream, milk, eggs and granulated sugar until warmed and the sugar is dissolved, being careful not to scramble the eggs.

Add the chocolate chips and cocoa powder, stirring until the chocolate is melted and thoroughly combined. Remove the pan from the heat and stir in the salt and vanilla. Place the bread cubes in an even layer in the prepared baking pan and pour the chocolate mixture evenly over the bread. Press down where necessary, to make sure all the bread is submerged. Cover the pan with plastic wrap and allow it to rest for 30 minutes so the mixture has time to absorb into the bread.

Set up the EGG for 350°F (180°C), indirect without a drip pan. Fill your firebox with natural lump charcoal and with the top and bottom vents wide open, light the fire and close the EGG. After about 10 minutes, close the bottom draft screen. When the temperature nears your 350°F (180°C) target temperature, partially close the bottom vent door and the top of the daisy wheel, leaving both vents 30 percent open. Make minor adjustments as necessary.

Once the grill comes up to temperature, place the pan of bread pudding on the cooking grid, close the lid and bake until the custard is set, 35 to 40 minutes. Remove the pan from the grill and let it rest for 5 minutes. Serve the bread pudding warm with a drizzle of the rum sauce.

Key Lime Pie with Graham Cracker Crust

Makes 8 servings

This Key lime pie has a rich and creamy filling that is complemented by a flavorful cookie crust. It has the perfect balance of sweet and tart, with just the right amount of zing.

CRUST

1½ cups (135 g) graham cracker crumbs

¼ cup (60 g) packed light brown sugar

Pinch of salt

7 tbsp (98 g) unsalted butter, melted

FILLING

3 large egg yolks

1 (14-oz [414-ml]) can sweetened condensed milk

⅔ cup (160 ml) bottled Key lime juice, such as Nellie & Joe's brand

FRESH WHIPPED CREAM

1 cup (240 ml) heavy cream, cold

2 tbsp (16 g) confectioners' sugar

½ tsp pure vanilla extract

GARNISH

Lime zest

Chill the bowl and whisk attachment of a stand mixer by placing them in the freezer for 15 minutes. Using cold cream and chilled equipment ensures that your cream will whip up faster and lighter.

Set up the EGG for 350°F (180°C), indirect without a drip pan. Fill your firebox with natural lump charcoal and with the top and bottom vents wide open, light the fire and close the EGG. After about 10 minutes, close the bottom draft screen. When the temperature nears your 350°F (180°C) target temperature, partially close the bottom vent door and the top of the daisy wheel, leaving both vents 30 percent open. Make minor adjustments as necessary.

Prepare the crust: In a medium-sized bowl, stir together the graham cracker crumbs, brown sugar and salt. Mix well to ensure no lumps remain in the brown sugar. Drizzle the melted butter over the graham cracker mixture and toss to combine with a fork, ensuring that the butter is evenly incorporated. Press the crust mixture evenly into the bottom and up the sides of an ungreased 9-inch (23-cm) pie plate.

Once the grill comes up to temperature, place the pie plate on the grate and close the lid. Bake for 10 minutes, then transfer the crust to a rack to cool.

Prepare the filling: In a medium-sized bowl, whisk the egg yolks until they become lighter in color and slightly thicker, 3 to 4 minutes. Add the sweetened condensed milk and lime juice, whisking until smooth. Pour the filling into the prepared crust and place the pan back on the cooking grate. Close the lid and bake for 10 to 12 minutes, or until the filling is just set. Remove the pie from the grill and place it on a rack to cool. Once cooled, refrigerate for 2 to 3 hours before serving it.

Prepare the whipped cream: In the bowl of a stand mixer fitted with the whisk attachment, whisk the cream on high speed until it begins to thicken, about 2 minutes. Add the confectioners' sugar and vanilla and continue to beat until stiff peaks form.

To serve: Slice and garnish the pie with whipped cream and lime zest.

Salted Chocolate Chunk Cookies

Makes 18 to 20 servings

Chocolate chunk cookies baked on the grill? Yes, please! Cooking with the lid closed, the Big Green Egg acts as an outdoor oven, providing a constant, even heat that is perfect for baking. These addictive cookies have just the right balance of salty and sweet in every bite. The coarse sea salt serves to intensify the flavor of the melty chunks of chocolate and is the finishing touch that will have you reaching for another one.

2¼ cups (281 g) all-purpose flour

½ tsp baking soda

1 tsp salt

1 cup (225 g/2 sticks) unsalted butter, at room temperature

1 cup (225 g) packed light brown sugar

½ cup (100 g) granulated sugar

2 tsp (10 ml) pure vanilla extract

2 large eggs

2 cups (350 g) dark or semisweet chocolate chunks

Coarse sea salt, for dusting

Cold milk, for serving

In a small bowl, whisk together the flour, baking soda and salt. Set aside.

In the bowl of a stand mixer fitted with the paddle attachment, beat the butter and both sugars on medium speed until light and fluffy, about 2 minutes. Reduce the speed to low and add the vanilla and eggs, mixing until combined, about 1 minute. Use a silicone spatula to scrape down the sides of the bowl. Add the flour mixture, one-third at a time, stirring until just combined. Stir in the chocolate chunks. Cover and refrigerate the dough for 30 minutes.

For each cookie, scoop about ¼ cup (60 g) of the dough and roll it into a ball. Place the balls of cookie dough 2 inches (5 cm) apart on an ungreased sheet pan. Using the palm of your hand, gently press down to slightly flatten the balls. Refrigerate for 30 minutes, or until you're ready to bake.

Set up the EGG to cook at 350°F (180°C), indirect without a drip pan. Fill your firebox with natural lump charcoal. With the top and bottom vents wide open, light the fire and close the lid. After about 10 minutes, close the bottom draft screen. As the dome temperature approaches your target temperature of 350°F (180°C), about 5 minutes, partially close the bottom vent door and the top of the daisy wheel, leaving both vents 30 percent open. Make minor adjustments as necessary.

Once the cooker is up to temperature, place the cookies on the grill and close the lid. Bake until the edges are golden and the centers are just set, 12 to 14 minutes. Remove from the grill and immediately sprinkle each cookie with a pinch of coarse sea salt. Allow the cookies to cool in their pan for a few minutes before transferring them to a wire rack.

Serve the cookies warm with a cold glass of milk.

Apple-Pear Crisp
with Oatmeal Crumb Topping
Makes 6 servings

This home-style crisp is perfect when you are craving a warm and comforting dessert. It is loaded with tender baked apples and pears, spiced with cinnamon, and topped with an irresistible brown sugar and oat crunch.

Butter, for greasing the skillet

FILLING

2 to 3 large Granny Smith apples, peeled, cored and diced (about 4 cups [600 g])

2 to 3 medium-sized ripe pears, peeled, cored and diced (about 2 cups [300 g])

2 tbsp (15 g) all-purpose flour

2 tbsp (26 g) granulated sugar

½ tsp ground cinnamon

1 tbsp (15 ml) fresh lemon juice

OATMEAL TOPPING

1 cup (80 g) old-fashioned oats

1 cup (125 g) all-purpose flour

¾ cup (169 g) packed light brown sugar

½ tsp ground cinnamon

¼ tsp salt

¾ cup (167 g/1½ sticks) unsalted butter, melted

Vanilla ice cream, to serve (optional)

Butter a 10-inch (25-cm) cast-iron skillet, then set aside.

Set up the EGG to cook at 350°F (180°C), indirect with a drip pan. Fill your firebox with natural lump charcoal. With the top and bottom vents wide open, light the fire and close the lid. After about 10 minutes, close the bottom draft screen. As the dome temperature approaches your target temperature of 350°F (180°C), about 5 minutes, partially close the bottom vent door and the top of the daisy wheel, leaving both vents 30 percent open. Make minor adjustments as necessary.

Prepare the filling: In a large bowl, stir together the apples, pears, flour, granulated sugar, cinnamon and lemon juice. Pour the filling into the prepared skillet.

Prepare the oatmeal topping: In a medium-sized bowl, combine the oats, flour, brown sugar, cinnamon and salt. Stir in the melted butter. Using your hands, work the topping into large crumbles. Sprinkle evenly over the fruit, covering the fruit completely.

Once the grill comes up to temperature, place the skillet on the grate and close the lid. Bake until the top is browned and the fruit is bubbly, 40 to 50 minutes. Remove the crisp from the grill and let it cool for a few minutes.

Serve the crisp warm with a scoop of vanilla ice cream, if desired.

MIXED BERRY COBBLER

Makes 12 to 15 servings

Since moving to a more rural part of our home state, my family and I have been exploring the many family-run u-pick farms. We have discovered an abundance of fresh produce—berries— right in our backyard. This berry cobbler is the perfect showcase for those amazing summer fruits. It is quick and easy to put together, and cooking it on the EGG results in a buttery, cakey bite that is bursting with jamlike fruit.

½ cup (112 g/1 stick) unsalted butter

1½ cups (188 g) all-purpose flour

1½ cups (300 g) sugar, plus 2 tbsp (26 g) for topping, divided

2 tsp (9 g) baking powder

½ tsp salt

1½ cups (355 ml) milk

4 cups (580 g) mixed berries, fresh or frozen

TOPPINGS (OPTIONAL)

Fresh whipped cream or vanilla ice cream

Set up the EGG to cook at 350°F (180°C), indirect without a drip pan. Fill your firebox with natural lump charcoal. With the top and bottom vents wide open, light the fire and close the lid. After about 10 minutes, close the bottom draft screen. As the dome temperature approaches your target temperature of 350°F (180°C), about 5 minutes, partially close the bottom vent door and the top of the daisy wheel, leaving both vents 30 percent open. Make minor adjustments as necessary.

Once the cooker comes up to temperature, place a 9 x 13–inch (23 x 33–cm) baking dish on the EGG. Place the butter in the pan to melt. Meanwhile, in a medium-sized bowl, whisk together the flour, 1½ cups (300 g) of sugar, the baking powder and salt. Add the milk, whisking to form a smooth batter.

Pour the batter over the melted butter in the pan. Scatter the mixed berries evenly over the batter and sprinkle with the remaining 2 tablespoons (26 g) of sugar.

Close the lid and bake until the batter is golden brown and the fruit is bubbling, 50 to 60 minutes, or until a toothpick inserted into the center comes out clean.

Dish out the cobbler while it is still warm and top it with whipped cream or vanilla ice cream, if desired.

GIANT CINNAMON ROLL
with BOURBON CREAM CHEESE FROSTING
Makes about 6 servings

This sweet and sticky cinnamon roll is the ultimate weekend brunch treat. The bourbon-infused topping has notes of vanilla and caramel that pair perfectly with the cinnamon and sugar in this sweet roll, making it an excellent choice for an indulgent dessert.

Nonstick spray

DOUGH

¼ cup (60 ml) warm water (105°F [41°C])

1 (0.25-oz [7-g]) package active dry yeast

½ cup (100 g) plus 1 tsp granulated sugar, divided

½ cup (120 ml) warmed milk (105°F [41°C])

2 large eggs

1 tsp salt

6 tbsp (84 g/¾ stick) unsalted butter, melted

4 to 4¼ cups (500 to 530 g) all-purpose flour, plus more for dusting

FILLING

½ cup (112 g/1 stick) unsalted butter, at room temperature

¾ cup (169 g) packed dark brown sugar

2 tbsp (14 g) ground cinnamon

FROSTING

4 oz (115 g) cream cheese, at room temperature

¼ cup (55 g/½ stick) unsalted butter, at room temperature

2 cups (240 g) confectioners' sugar

1 tsp pure vanilla extract

1 tbsp (15 ml) bourbon

1 tbsp (15 ml) milk

Spray a large bowl with nonstick spray, then set aside.

Prepare the dough: In the bowl of a stand mixer fitted with the paddle attachment, combine the water, yeast and 1 teaspoon of granulated sugar. Let the mixture sit until foamy, 2 to 3 minutes. Add the milk, eggs, remaining ½ cup (100 g) of granulated sugar, salt, butter and 4 cups (500 g) of the flour to the bowl. Mix on low speed until a dough forms, 1 to 2 minutes.

Switch the mixer to the dough hook attachment and knead the dough until it is smooth and elastic, 4 to 5 minutes. Adjust the stickiness of the dough by adding more flour, 1 tablespoon (8 g) at a time, until the dough is easy to handle and not overly sticky.

Form the dough into a ball and place it in the prepared bowl. Spray the top of the dough with nonstick spray and cover it with plastic wrap. Let the dough rise in a warm place until it is doubled in size, about 1½ hours.

While the dough is rising, prepare the filling: In a small bowl, stir together the butter, brown sugar and cinnamon. Set aside.

Prepare the frosting: In the bowl of the stand mixer fitted with the paddle attachment, beat the cream cheese and butter on medium speed until creamy, 3 to 4 minutes. Reduce the speed to low and gradually add the confectioners' sugar, beating until fluffy. Stir in the vanilla, bourbon and milk until just combined, then set aside.

Spray a 10-inch (25-cm) cast-iron skillet with nonstick spray, then set aside.

(continued)

On a lightly floured surface, roll out the dough to a 12 x 18–inch (30 x 45–cm) rectangle. Spread the filling to cover the dough. Using a pastry wheel or a pizza cutter, cut the dough into six 2-inch (5-cm)-wide strips. Tightly roll one strip of dough into a spiral, then place it in the center of the prepared skillet. Wrap the remaining strips of dough around the spiral in the skillet.

Cover the pan with plastic wrap and let the dough rise in a warm place until the dough puffs up to reach the top of the skillet, about 45 minutes.

Set up the EGG for 350°F (180°C), indirect without a drip pan. Fill your firebox with natural lump charcoal and with the top and bottom vents wide open, light the fire and close the EGG. After about 10 minutes, close the bottom draft screen. When the temperature nears your 350°F (180°C) target temperature, partially close the bottom vent door and the top of the daisy wheel, leaving both vents 30 percent open. Make minor adjustments as necessary.

Once the EGG comes up to temperature, uncover the pan and place it on the cooking grate. Close the lid and bake until the cinnamon roll is golden brown and a wooden toothpick inserted in the center comes out clean, about 45 minutes. Remove the cinnamon roll from the grill and allow it to cool for 5 minutes. Spread the frosting on the warm cinnamon roll to serve.

ACKNOWLEDGMENTS

This book would not have been possible without the support, hard work and dedication of the many talented people who assisted with its creation. I would like to thank . . .

My wife, Kelly Sheehan, for giving me the support and encouragement to always follow my dreams, no matter what.

My son, Raymond Stuart Sheehan, for taking on additional chores so that I could write without interruption, and for assisting with the photo shoot.

My mom, Lucille, and my sister, Kristine, for their love and encouragement.

Will Kiester, my publisher, and Marissa Giambelluca, my editor, for believing in me and giving me the opportunity to write another book. To the exceptional team at Page Street Publishing for bringing this book to life and guiding me through the process.

Ken Goodman, you don't just take great photographs, you make them! Thank you for your vision, patience, humor and extraordinary talent.

Stewart Goldstein at Monmouth Meats, and New Egypt Marketplace for the amazing meats, produce and groceries used for the photo shoot.

The team that keeps our BBQ Buddha brand running, Glenn Vandervort, Tim Citrone, Brian Garrett, Mark Joseph Kelly, Brian Leigh, Jenny Mann and Mann Made Creative. Whether it is working events, picking up product, assisting with photo shoots, taste testing, creating labels or web design, you guys rock!

Kell and Janet Phelps at *Barbecue News Magazine*, Sean Ludwig and Ryan Cooper at The Smoke Sheet and Janna Renfro and Jane Ehrhardt at *Tailgater Magazine*, for all your support and for featuring my recipes, articles and books.

David Malek at Gunter Wilhelm, for the amazing cutlery and cookware.

Love to my Cravings family, for making this journey that much sweeter—Jan, Stu, Kate, Sheri and DJ.

About the Author

Ray Sheehan is the author of *Award-Winning BBQ Sauces and How to Use Them* and the founder and owner of BBQ Buddha, an international award-winning line of healthy-minded BBQ sauces and rubs. He is also the Pit Master for the BBQ Buddha Competition team and a certified Kansas City Barbeque Society judge. Ray spends his time running the day-to-day operations of the business, but his true passions are creating award-winning BBQ products and teaching others how to use them. His sauces have won numerous awards at some of the biggest sauce contests, including the American Royal "Best Sauce on the Planet" contest, the Scovie Awards, the National Barbecue and Grilling Association's Awards of Excellence, the International Artisan Flavor Awards (the Flaves), the World Hot Sauce Awards and the Sauce King NYC Grand Championship.

A chef by trade, Ray has been in the food business for over 25 years. Since 2017, he has been a contributor to *Barbecue News Magazine*, providing recipes, articles and product reviews. Ray has appeared on PA Live! WBRE-NBC; Food and Wine with Chef Jamie Gwen; Talk Radio 790 KABC, Los Angeles; Barbecue Nation with JT AM 860 KPAM; Smoking Hot Confessions BBQ Podcast, Australia; The BBQ Talks Show, United Kingdom; The BBQ Beat Podcast; The Pit Life BBQ Podcast; Beer Sessions Radio on the Heritage Radio Network; Dining on a Dime 103.7 FM New York; and Small Bites with Donato Marino & Derek Timm, the #1-listed "Food Radio Show in Philadelphia."

Ray has been featured in *Tailgater Magazine*, The Smoke Sheet BBQ newsletter, *Edible Jersey* magazine, *New Jersey Monthly* magazine, *Industry* magazine, the *Asbury Park Press* and the *Coaster* newspaper. He lives in New Egypt, New Jersey, with his wife, Kelly, son, Raymond and dogs Serena and Sammy.

For more information about Ray's award-winning BBQ products, please visit www.bbqbuddha.com.

To connect with Ray on social media:

- Facebook: https://facebook.com/awardwinningbbqsauce
- Instagram: www.instagram.com/bbq_buddha
- Twitter: http://twitter.com/bbq_buddha

INDEX